End

This book serves as a reminder that nothing can destroy the destiny that God has for us. The testimony of God's faithfulness in the lives of the Bradford brothers confirms that God uses tragedy and triumph to fulfill His purpose in our lives.

Pastor John Ragsdale
The Hills
Nashville, TN

Jordan Bradford is an anointed preacher, teacher, writer and musician. He is a gift to the body of Christ. I have known him for years. I can honestly say that he is a man of integrity in EVERY area of ministry. He has a passion to reach his generation with the Gospel. That passion is contagious. Connect with this ministry. As you do, you will see increase in your own life.

Terry Tripp
Terry Tripp Ministries
Hendersonville, TN

Jordan Bradford is both a breath of fresh air and a bolt of lightening in one package. I have found his passion to help people to be insightful, inspirational and challenging. Jordan is a young man whose energy and enthusiasm leave an indelible impression and lasting impact on everyone he encounters.

Pastor Rob Yanok
GraceTown Church
Columbus, Ohio

Jordan Bradford is a voice for this generation, an anointed man of God that is not afraid to speak the truth in love. I highly recommend the ministry of Jordan Bradford.

Pastor Robb Tripp
The Fire Place Fellowship
Hendersonville, TN

Jordan Bradford is laden with many wonderful God-given gifts. His innovative musical abilities and his inspired verve in speaking, along with his command of the Scriptural truths, make him a propitious influence on the body of Christ.

Pastor Chuck Lawrence
Christ Temple Church
Huntington, WV

Our world is in desperate need of anointed leaders, fresh from an 'Inferno Experience.' Biblically-sound and Spirit-led, the pen of the author, Jordan Bradford, captures an essential understanding...that all great leaders are forged in the fires of adversity. This book will challenge you to stand firm in the face of secularism, to rise from the throes of failure, and to capture your passionate purpose for living. You will be inspired to discover your God-assignment via the heat of trials. Great leaders are tested before they are trusted...broken before they are blessed. I whole-heartedly recommend to you 'The Inferno Experience.'

Pastor Tim Estes
New Life Tabernacle
Siloam Springs, AR

I had the amazing opportunity to meet Jordan Bradford this past year, and what an incredible guy! His heart for God and God's people is unending. His talent and charisma are charged with God's love. What I like most about Jordan is his ability to hear God's voice and do whatever it takes to obey, no matter the cost. Jordan Bradford is a world-changer!

Pastor John Brockman
Worship Pastor
Destiny World Outreach Center
Killeen, TX

Jordan Bradford possesses an authentic and undeniable zeal for God, and his continual push for righteousness is absolutely contagious. He is driven by an insatiable hunger to see Christ lifted high in the earth, and he and his brother's music reflects this with lyrics that exalt the Lord and inspire worship within individual hearts across the country. When they write a song, its sole purpose is to make Christ famous and set His people free. In the time I've been privileged to know Jordan, he has treated me not only as a friend but as family. His example inspires others to dive deeper in God as he truly exemplifies the love of Christ in all he does.

Daniel Johnson
Gospel Recording Artist
Worship Leader, New Breed Music

THE INFERNO EXPERIENCE

THAT WHICH CHANGES A NATION
AND SHAPES A GENERATION

JORDAN BRADFORD

BB

BRADFORD & BRADFORD
PUBLISHING

The following versions of Scripture are cited in this book:
KJV, NIV, NLT, ERV, AMP, ESV, HCSB

Cover design by iDesign Professional Graphic Web Design
Cover photograph by dreamstime.com

Interior design by
iDesign Professional Graphic Web Design
Interior historical photographs by dreamstime.com

Published by Bradford and Bradford Publishing
P.O. Box 206
Middleport, OH 45760
www.bradfordministries.net

Bradford and Bradford Publishing is a division of Bradford
Ministries, Nashville, TN

Dedication

It is a great honor to dedicate this book to my parents and pastors, Michael and Kimberly Bradford.

Chapter/Section Titles

PREFACE

Contained within the confines of this book are numerous writing styles, tactics and dimensions of literature, each varying from the other in depth, demeanor and disposition. This I have acknowledged and qualified as acceptable as I have set to present to you, not a literary masterpiece, but rather a practical guide to seeking, seeing and remaining in the face of Almighty God. It is my utmost belief that there is but one possession man is capable of transporting from this temporary life into the life of eternity, that being the wisdom and integrity gained through the accumulation of moments spent in companionship and communion with Father God who is the only one able to search and know even the deepest parts of each man's heart.

God is an all-consuming fire. Deuteronomy 4:24: *"For the Lord your God is a consuming Fire, a jealous God."* And again, in Hebrews 12:29: *"For our God is an all-consuming Fire."* Many have experienced the outermost part of the presence of God known as the anointing. Countless others have even received the Holy Spirit, which is ever so important; however, it is my desire to see all that will experience the Fire of Almighty God.

Mathew chapter 3 and verse 11
I indeed baptize you with water unto repentance: but He that comes after me is mightier than I, whose shoes I am not worthy to bear: He shall baptize you with the Holy Spirit, and with Fire.

(KJV)

And the beginning of the fulfillment, Acts 2:3: *"Then what looked like flames of fire appeared to them and settled on each of them."*

This book holds the answers to some of today's most colossal and important questions, questions not only demanding an answer from the Body of Christ, but questions also facing this great America and the world as a whole. I believe the answers to today's most pressing challenges are contained in one answer manifested as the generation foretold from the heart of David, a man after the face of God.

Psalms chapter 24 and verses 5-6
(5.) That generation will receive the Lord's blessing and have a right relationship with their savior.

(6.) Such is the generation of those who seek Him, who seek Your Face O God. The very God of the covenant of Jacob.

(NIV)

There is a place in God in which even the deepest of fears are removed, and in their place left to remain is the mark of God containing the goodness, the wisdom, and the love for God. This writing is designed to be a manual for the seeker of His Face, a road map, while in part, for all who would dare to journey to the place of His Fire.

This book will help you launch into a dimension of glory in which is contained the secrets to shape generations, change nations and birth a spiritual awakening unlike any the world has ever known. If you find this book in your hand, you will soon discover or rediscover the capacity to reach for all that is promised you.

Let us begin.

FOREWORD

This book that you now hold in your hands will inspire your heart and ignite you to a dimension of relationship with All-Mighty God like you have never experienced before!

Pastor Jordan Bradford has definitely heard from God with the writing of this book and is indeed...Shaping a Generation through his ministry!

Sincerely,
Dr. Michael Chitwood
General Overseer
International Congress of Churches & Ministers

MY STORY

Everything about our time in Ohio over the previous two years had been nothing short of a miracle from God. The very fact that we found ourselves living in a northern American town was completely unexpected. I was born and raised in a small town in Northeast Arkansas and had, at one point, planned to spend the entirety of my days there. I thought I knew the exact path my life would take, and I had each detail meticulously mapped out. I was raised in the south, and in the south I would stay. Then, the Lord stepped in, and after short stints of full-time ministry in small towns in two different states, my family and I found ourselves in rural southeastern Ohio, taking on a new challenge. My father had accepted the pastorate of a church there, and through the power of the Holy Spirit, we were seeing the Lord change and soften the hearts of many of our parishioners while simultaneously drawing in passionate, new members, all eager to see the message of the Gospel spread to the surrounding community.

The Lord had spoken a specific instruction to me and my brother Isaac the previous year, and although we were unsure of how to accomplish this monumental task, we knew the Lord had spoken. We decided to move forward with what was within our ability to do. The church, prior to our arrival, had purchased an old bar that was situated next door to our sanctuary, and in 2006, it sat empty. In a time of prayer that year, the Lord spoke to us very clearly to convert this building into a place for the young people of the area to assemble and encounter the Lord in powerful ways. There was no other positive influence in our small town for young people, and the severe poverty and lack of opportunity in this northernmost region of Appalachia left many young people with little hope.

We had no money, but we did have a word from the Lord, a few hammers, and strong backs. We set to work tearing out the entire interior of the old bar. What would happen when we had emptied it out, we weren't sure, but we knew that He had promised that He would do what *only* He could do once we had done all that we could do. As we were finishing the demolition, a woman unexpectedly appeared in  the front entrance one day, thrust something into my hand, and blurted out, *"I don't really know you, and I don't really like you. But, the Lord told me to give this to you."* She left abruptly, and I was completely stunned to find in my hand a check for $20,000! This same woman would later return and bless us with another $10,000, and with this money we began making plans to build a youth center for the Glory of God.

My brother and I provided most of the manpower on the project with the help of a few faithful young men from our congregation, so in June of 2007, we were still hard at work. One sunny morning, with the help of a local hardware store clerk, I purchased a chemical he said would help us remove carpet glue from the cement floor as we prepared to lay new flooring in what would soon be my new office. We all met up at the youth center and set to work. I poured the chemical onto the floor in one area of the room and left it as I work in another area, down on my hands and knees with a small grinder in my hand attempting to remove the stubborn glue from the bare concrete.

As I worked, I noticed a flickering light on the wall beside me, and as I turned to look, I realized that my boot was in flames. A spark had flown off my grinder and hit the chemical puddle on the floor that my boot was resting in, catching the small area on fire. I immediately stood up and worked to stamp out the flames, concerned mostly at this point with avoiding costly damages to the freshly painted walls. Before I knew it, however, my leg was in flames up to my knee. Realizing the escalating danger, I hurried out into the hallway as I searched for a way to put out the flames. The added oxygen only put me in even more dyer straights as the flames reached my waist. Almost in a panic, I jumped outside where my brother was

17

painting a door, and instantly, the flames shot higher, covering my entire body.

I could manage only a quiet, "Help!" as I staggered from the building. I fell to the ground, running into my car which was parked just outside the door as I went down, and my brother quickly grabbed the carpet that had previously been in the office where I was working and threw it over me. When he removed the carpet again, the flames reignited. He covered me back up and waited several minutes until we were sure that the flames had been completely smothered out.

I knew I was badly hurt, but I was determined to stay calm and was even planning to return to work in order to keep those there working with us calm and assured. As they helped me to my feet, we began making our way back into the building. As we re-entered the hallway, the pain in my right leg suddenly seized me, and I began shaking uncontrollably. They helped me sit down and remove my jeans. My brother now often tells the story of how he felt as he removed my jeans and watched the skin of my lower right leg literally peel off with them.

My mother soon arrived, and with much assistance, I managed to climb into the front seat of her SUV. We sped on to the nearest hospital as I drifted in and out of consciousness due to the unimaginable pain pulsing through my leg. They took me directly into the ER, but the small hospital was not aptly equipped to handle my case, performing excruciatingly painful procedures on my leg that we learned later had not been widely used in the field of medicine for nearly fifty years. They then explained to me that I had only first-degree burns and that I was fine. I should simply go home and rest, soaking my leg every four hours.

Trusting this instruction, we went home. I lay down on the couch, and we placed a number of towels beneath my leg. I was still delirious from the immense pain, and I was losing so much fluid through my burn that we couldn't keep dry towels beneath me. The fluid was seeping through them and onto the couch. We finally called The Ohio State University Medical Center, whose burn unit is nationally recognized, and explained my injuries. They urged us to make the two-hour trip to their facility in Columbus immediately. They later explained to us that had we waited until the following morning, I most likely would not have made it through the night due mostly to the drastic loss of fluid my body had suffered.

The burns on my lower right leg had in fact been mostly first-degree with some second-degree in severity, but because the fire that had erupted against my skin was chemical in nature, the chemicals that had made contact with my bare leg had continued to burn my flesh even after the flames were extinguished until my entire leg from my knee to just below my ankle and across the top of my foot was covered in one solid, third-degree burn.

The following day, as I prepared for surgery, I signed a paper giving doctors permission to amputate my leg if the damage proved irreparable. They wheeled me into surgery, and although they were able to salvage my leg, the doctor was certain that walking would be very difficult for me and that running would forever be completely out of the question because my Achilles' tendon was irrevocably destroyed. During the surgery, the doctors removed all remaining skin along with large portions of muscle from my leg and performed a skin graft, shaving off long sheets of skin from both of my thighs and wrapping my lower leg in them. I was an experiment of sorts because I had entered the hospital with the largest circumferential burn that the OSU Medical Center had ever encountered, and they were unsure if such a large, complex graft would be successful.

Because no portion of my lower leg was unaffected, there was no way for me to lay it against the sheets of my hospital bed without completely ruining the graft; therefore, as part of my surgery, the doctor drilled two holes into my shinbone and anchored two small metal rods in the bone. These rods were attached to poles above the foot of my bed which suspended my leg in mid-air. My right leg was literally hanging by my shinbone.

I spent three weeks in the burn unit, battling unimaginable pain. I had to take pain medication every two hours, making restful sleep an impossibility. I was also forced to stop taking my most powerful pain reliever because it was causing terrifying hallucinations and making it impossible for me to think clearly. In addition to the pain of having had my leg literally skinned and stripped down to nearly nothing, the metal rods protruding from my leg sent sharp pains through my bone with even the tiniest of movements.

The doctors and nurses attempted on several occasions to pronounce a hopeless prognosis over me, but we were quick to dismiss such statements, and if necessary the medical professionals who were insistent that I hear them, and we chose instead to throw ourselves wholeheartedly at the feet of the Master knowing our shelter was in His arms. We certainly had learned over our years of serving the Lord

how to call on His Name and stand in faith, believing Him to do the miraculous. I attempted on several occasions to read my Bible, but the combination of my medications and the blinding pain made it essentially impossible to focus on the text. My family would take turns reading the Word to me in short spurts until I would drift off into unconsciousness, and we spent a large part of our time in the hospital in prayer. I also played repeatedly a DVD of Grammy-Award Winning gospel artist Israel Houghton and New Breed performing the live recording of their *Alive in South Africa* CD.

My family and I had made plans to travel to Pastor Rod Parsley's World Harvest Church in Columbus, Ohio, on the fourth of July weekend that year to be a part of their annual camp meeting. We were in Columbus that weekend, but

we were not gathered around the altar of this great church but instead around the hospital bed turned makeshift altar that

we had created in my room. One day the following week, my mother decided to call World Harvest and see if they would be willing to send us a DVD recording of the camp meeting so that we could experience the service in some small way. We had no idea that the Lord was about to rain extreme favor upon us in completely unexpected ways.

After my mother's phone call, my story soon spread throughout the World Harvest ministerial staff. One afternoon, I looked up to see Elder Ronnie Harrison, senior elder of World Harvest Church, standing in the doorway of my hospital room.  He explained to us that when he heard my story, the Lord spoke to him and told him that he needed to come and see me at OSU. We had an incredible visit, with the Lord stirring and moving in our midst in miraculous ways, and before he left, Elder Ronnie offered me a full-ride scholarship to World Harvest Bible College (now Valor Christian College). Was it possible that the Lord moved this young southern boy from Arkansas to Ohio and placed me in that hospital room, not as an enemy attack, but as a launching pad to propel me into my destiny?

Eventually, I was discharged from the hospital, with a determination to return to the same physical shape I had been in prior to my accident. I did walk again, and as a matter of fact, my brother and I walked together into a lecture hall of the great World Harvest Bible College together that September, backed by two God-given, full-ride scholarships and great favor from Almighty God. Within one year, I was in my tennis shoes and on the track running up to three miles at a time, and through the power of the Lord, I was beating all odds stacked against me.

We attended college during the week and returned home on the weekends, continuing work on the conversion of our old bar. Our youth center, The Inferno, in a town with less than 2,000 total population, opened its doors in May of 2008 with over two hundred young people in attendance, many encountering Christ for the

Pastor Jordan and his youth group filming an Inferno video.

first time. The Inferno Youth Ministry went on to impact countless young lives in the years that followed, reaching out to children in the local community, surrounding communities, and eventually in other states.

During our time at World Harvest, my brother and I were blessed to play on the platform of World Harvest Church and Next Harvest Youth Church, and we played in and also led the chapel band for World Harvest Bible College. We played for Pastor Rod and for his mother, Ellen Parsley, on a regular basis and were employed by the church for some time. Our time at WHBC provided us opportunities to make connections that carried us to churches across America and as far away as Kimberley, South Africa, where the Lord enabled us to minister to thousands.

My mother wrote a letter in 2008 to Israel Houghton, explaining to him the irreplaceable role his music had played in my recovery and thanking him for setting his life to carry the Gospel to the lost and the hurting. Israel immediately contacted us, and we made a connection that year at a church in Toledo. We joined him in the green room after service and shared both our story and our hunger for the presence of the Lord, and he shared so much with us and poured priceless wisdom and encouragement into our lives.

Youth Conference

He later paid our way to Texas to be a part of his Deeper Level 2009 Conference the following year where I was given the opportunity to speak before thousands of people, sharing my story along with a powerful word that the Lord gave me concerning *THE* Fire as I encountered *a* fire and recovered from its wrath only two short years before. This is the same message I've penned in this book and am eager to share with those hungry for a physical manifestation of the Spirit of the Lord. If you count yourself in this number, please read on and understand that if you are truly ready to see Christ arrest a people, an entire nation, your road map to the most secret, intimate encounters with Almighty God is at your fingertips. It's time to experience the Fire.

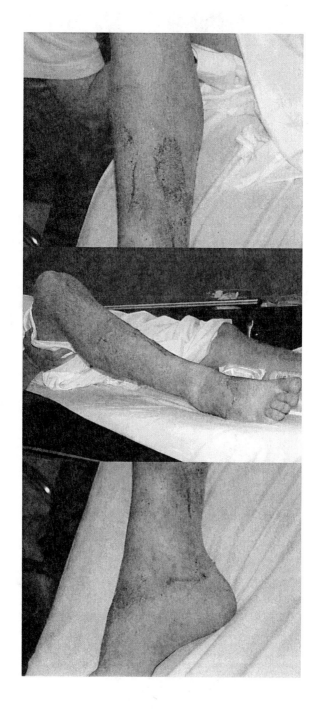

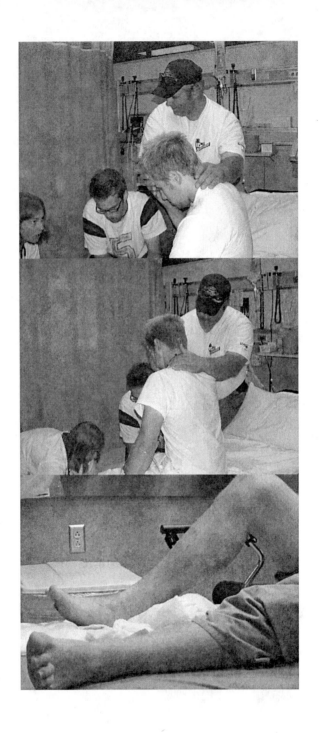

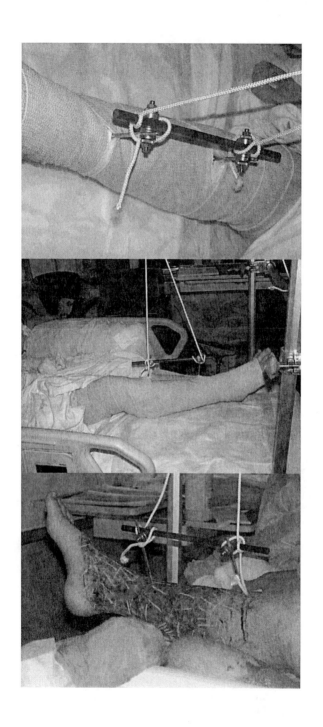

Aaron Lindsey

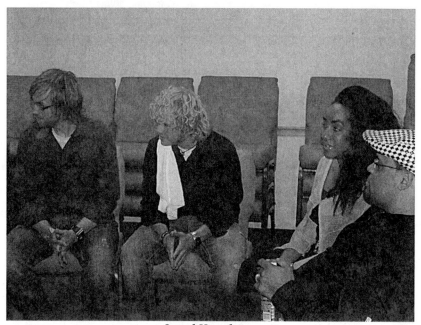

Israel Houghton

Ricardo Sanchez

Sidney Mohede

Israel Houghton

WHBC/Valor Christian College

Peter Wilson

Barry Southgate

Lisa Brunson

William McDowell

Sam Hinn

Darlene Zschech

Israel Houghton

David Binion

Ellen Parsley

Jerry Harris

CHAPTER

THE ENEMY'S OBJECTIVE

Whether you realize it or not, you are engaged in a war: a war with the forces of hell, a war with the enemy of your soul. In fact, it's an age-old war. This war is waged in an invisible world with invisible tactics; however, the ramifications of this war are directly affecting and totally dictating the events of the VISIBLE world. So in other words, though you may not see actual bullets whizzing by or feel mortars exploding nearby, though you may not physically see or hear the enemy troops advancing on your position, this doesn't diminish the startling truth that the effects of this war are apparent all around. Each time you see a marriage on the rocks, with two people once so in love now going their separate ways, you've seen the fingerprint of the enemy. As you look around and see people created in the image of God, made in His very likeness, destroying their bodies through the use of drugs, alcohol, cutting and other vile practices of self-destruction or addiction, you see his scheming in action. At the heart of these behaviors, it's not that these individuals seek to

37

destroy their relationships or their bodies. Actually quite the contrary is true. Each person is born with a desire from God to care for and pro-create themselves (Genesis 1:28). However, people turn to these very destructive devises as a method of dealing and coping with inner wounds left in the soulish area of a person and are the aftermath and real evidence of an unseen war that in some way, at some time, comes to us all.

But, don't just take my word for it. Let's get to God's Word and see what He has to say on the matter. First, in Genesis 1:28 (referenced above), it says:

*"And God blessed them, and God said unto them, Be fruitful, and multiply, and replenish the earth, and **subdue it**: and **have dominion over** the fish of the sea, and over the fowl of the air, and over every living thing that moveth upon the earth."*

(KJV, emphasis mine)

In order to subdue something, we must first cause, through contentious struggle or war on some level, the opposing party, person, animal or object, to come into submission. Or you may say that in order to subdue it, we must first submit it. Dominion is not achieved by merit alone. There is a process by which one comes to rule or govern another. Yes, it's true that like you and I, Adam was a son of God; however, Adam still had to actively attend to the very real threats that opposed him. There was still a process of struggle or war that had to be addressed regularly.

Ephesians chapter 6 beginning in verse 10 and continuing through verse 18 bears this out in vivid detail. It reads:

(10.) "Finally, my brethren, be strong in the Lord, and in the power of his might..."

Verse 11 tells us why and then how we are to be strong.

*(11.) "Put on the whole **armor of God**, that ye may be able to **stand against** the wiles* (tactical plan of attack) *of the devil.*

(12.) For we wrestle not against flesh and blood, but (we) *wrestle* (FIGHT, COMBAT, STAND AGAINST) *principalities, against* (militant) *powers, against the rulers of the darkness of this world, against spiritual wickedness in high places.*

*(13.) Wherefore take unto you the **whole** armor of God, that ye may be able to withstand in the evil day, and having done all, to stand..."*

If you're going to be able to stand against, you must stand with the whole armor of God. Armor points to the anticipation of battle.

(14.) "Stand therefore, having your loins girted about with truth, and having on the breastplate of righteousness;

(15.) And your feet shod with the preparation of the gospel of peace;

(16.) Above all, taking the shield of faith, wherewith ye shall be able to quench all the fiery darts of the wicked.

(17.) And take the helmet of salvation, and the sword of the Spirit, which is the word of God:

(18.) Praying always with all prayer and supplication in the Spirit, and watching thereunto with all perseverance and supplication for all saints."

(KJV, emphasis and parenthetical notes mine)

Now let's stop to ponder this text and all that it implies. In this verse, we're talking about amour, swords, shields, and standing in the power and might of God himself. We don't need to be strong and ordained in the armor of God, standing in his strength, to make it through the routine, day-to-day rhythms of life. It doesn't take the armor of God to cook breakfast, drop your kids off at school, feed the dog, wash the car or update your Facebook status. The sword of the spirit and the armor of God aren't needed for the squabble you may be having with your spouse or the trouble you may be in with your parents. It isn't even needed for that occasional speeding ticket, flat tire, missing sock or traffic jam. The scriptures are clear. You have to be standing in the strength of God, having the whole armor of God, which He provides, in order to stand against or FIGHT the regimented, violent enemy in the person of the devil who is organized and cunning in his tactics.

It's also readily evident that the armor of God isn't for a select few or only for the pastor, worship pastor, church staff member or church leader. The armor of God is for every born-again Christian believer in every denomination from catholic to charismatic. The armor of God is necessary for every position of service in the Body of Christ from apostle to janitor, and for every age range from children's church child to lead elder. In fact, Paul is letting us know in these verses that there is a very real enemy, who is ready, willing and planning to fight with his objective being to distract, divert and destroy your destiny. The apostle and chief writer of the New Testament highlighted this fact, yet so many have missed it. That being said, there is a real war going on, a war in which all must engage. It is a war for your eternal soul and the destiny of your life. So the armor is in fact a clue to our first truth fact. This spiritual war is an all-inclusive war, one in which all must engage. Armor is for fighting, plain and simple. Swords are for war, and the strength of God is for standing against or defending all that God has placed you over.

The enemy's objective is to defeat, destroy and divert your destiny and eternal purpose. He plans to do this through aggressively, strategically causing you to forget or begin to reason the words of God, which are the promises of God. The enemy's agenda is to control your schedule, contort your circumstances and calm your God-given fighting spirit, all to cause you to give up on or abort your own destiny. It's true that the enemy cannot keep you from your destiny. However, if you are unaware of his tactics and consequently are unprepared and unarmed, you will be unable to weather the storm or attack of the enemy, and as a result you will simply give up on your destiny. If you remain unarmed and unprepared in prayer and fasting for the fight that is happening all around, in the heat of the storm, you'll give up on your destiny and fall to the subtle tactics of the devil, our adversary.

You are a son or daughter of God himself. He has great and mighty plans for your life. God has a specific purpose for you to fulfill. There is greatness in you. That's why there is a fight. The fight, the opposition, is evidence that there is greatness in you. The enemy is jealous and will stop at nothing... except a blood-bought, Spirit-filled man or woman of God that is armed and ready to speak the Word, standing day and night in the secret place to see the hand of God move, destroying the works of the devil.

IDENTITY CRISIS

There is a plague sweeping this nation, an epidemic so large in dimension that it has literally infiltrated every level of living. This plague troubles the lives of many, from those who find shelter from the elements under a piece of ragged cardboard or in an abandoned warehouse, to those living in the most elaborate mansions or palaces known to man. With some careful observation or a well-placed question, this blight against humanity becomes readily evident. You can find victims of its menacing attacks in every state, in every occupation and at every level of education and pedigree. It's no respecter of persons. This paralysis strikes every age, every body type, every gender. This plague: Identity Crisis.

The enemy looks to sow the destructive seeds of identity crisis early in the life of each person, as you will soon see in the after-mentioned definition of the term *identity crisis*. The root of the problem begins to form as early as the latter years of childhood but is sometimes seemingly unnoticed until later in life. *Identity crisis* as defined by Erik Erikson, a prominent Jewish psychologist who subsequently coined the phrase in the mid-late 20th century, is "a psychosocial state or condition of disorientation and role confusion occurring especially in adolescents as a result of conflicting internal experiences, pressures, and expectations."

Manifestations of Assault on Identity

Identity crisis often produces anxiety. Low self-esteem and low self-worth are often the signs of identity crisis. One who experiences identity crisis often turns to dangerous, delinquent and often self-destructive behavior. Actions like self-medicating, drug use, cutting and crime, as well as all types of mental, physical, verbal and sexual abuse stem from a loss of identity. Erickson went on to describe the direct results of the attack on one's identity. He states that those who are going through an identity crisis are experiencing inner turmoil on the highest of levels. Victims are confused and deranged, having no sense of self-purpose, self-value or self-worth. They, as a result, have no idea what they want to do with their lives, nor do they possess any sense of why they were created. Victims lack motivation and the will to pursue all that life has to offer. They are struggling in the depths of their souls, attempting to find themselves. In short, they have no idea who they are or why.

Answers to Some Major Questions

You see it takes more than "good raising" and honest parents to ensure that children will mature to fulfill their God-given purpose. You can grow up in a Christian family, attend church every week, and even attend a Christian school and still not know your purpose. This is why we often see ministry and Christian families with children who grow up and seemingly walk away from the faith; however, it's important to understand that this is not true only in Christian homes. We see the aftermath of identity crisis in the families of the mayor, the governor, even businessmen and blue-collar families as well. The rich and poor alike experience the effects of the war waged against this generation. Herein lies the crux of the matter. If your eyes are opened and your spirit enlarged to receive the next series of statements and revelations, you will become aware of the most divisive ways the enemy is assaulting this generation. This will answer questions like, *"How can a child grow up in the house of God and become gay, enter a life of sexual perversion, drug abuse, or even commit heinous crimes against humanity?"* Or, *"How can a husband, after many years, suddenly leave his family?"* Even, *"How can a pastor or church leader who knows the Word have an affair or an addiction problem?"*

Remember 2 Corinthians chapter 2 and verse 11, which warns us to:

"(be aware, study to know how) *Lest satan should get an advantage of us: for we are not ignorant* (as leaders, or apostles) *of his devices."*

(KJV, parenthetical notes mine)

The Purpose is Purpose

If you don't know who you are, you have no idea who you are to become. If you have no idea who you are to become, you have no idea what you're capable of. If you have no idea what you're capable of, it becomes very easy to throw away your future through any number of self-destructive means. The reason the enemy has launched an all-out attack on this generation is because I believe this is the generation prophesied about by King David. We find his insight concerning this generation in the Psalms:

Psalm chapter 24 and verse 6
"This is the generation of them that seek after HIM, that seek Thy Face, O God of Jacob."

(ERV)

This generation is about more than just living. It's about more than getting up, going to work, coming home, buying a nice house, earning a good wage, providing for a family and attending church on Sunday. For this generation, there has to be more. There is a longing within our spirits to discover what it's really all about, the proverbial "why" behind our existence, the reason things in life have turned out the way they did, the reason that *this* happened to me and the reason that *that* happened to me. People want to know the reason they were born where they were born, in the time they were born, to the family they were born. As a result of this longing in their spirits, people seemingly give up and throw in the towel. We read about and hear about it all the time. It's the person for whom it appeared that everything was going the right way.

Then suddenly something shifts, and they're a faint shadow of their former self. Why? It's because deep in the heart of each person is a longing to discover, to uncover, their God-given purpose.

Purpose is defined as, "the reason for which something exists or is made." The attack on identity is about purpose. This generation's purpose is so great both individually and collectively that the enemy has unleashed all his forces in an attempt to stop it while it remains in infancy, before there is time for each of us to gain an understanding of who we are because of WHOSE we are.

Here's the KEY

Until you know the reason for which you were made, you cannot know the *purpose* for which you were intended. Simply put, if you have nothing to aim at, you cannot hit the mark. So you see, the reason the enemy, satan our adversary, is attacking this generation's identity is because he is nervous that if left unscaved, this generation may have the time needed to gather ourselves and get a close look at our Daddy, or *Abba*. And if this generation ever gets a look at Who our Heavenly Father is, we will begin to look in the mirror of the Spirit, discover and declare, "I am made in the image of my Father. I am made like my Daddy, and if Daddy can do it, then I can do it. If my Father can destroy the works of the enemy, then I, through His authority as my Father, can destroy the works of the enemy."

In John 14:12, Jesus speaking, it says, *"I tell you the truth. Anyone who has faith in me will do what I have been doing. He* (that person) *will even do greater things than me because I am going to the Father"* (NIV, parenthetical notes mine). I believe this is the greatest generation ever to set foot upon Planet Earth. I believe this generation has a God mandate to, in the words of Riendhard Bonnke, "plunder hell and populate heaven." That's why there is an attack on your marriage. That's why you lost your job. That's why all hell has broken loose against your family. That's why your finances are going down the tubes and your health is faltering. It's not about you. It's about your purpose. You have a purpose that is greater than you have imagined.

But, as Scripture says, *"No eye has seen, no ear has heard, and no mind has **imagined** the things that God has prepared for those who love him"* (1 Corinthians 2:9, emphasis mine). No other person on earth was created like you. You have a fingerprint that is all your own. You have an iris within your eye that is unlike any other ever created. You have a specific set of DNA blueprints that is completely unique. God broke the mold when he made you. You're the only *you* that there will ever be. There's no competition. No matter how hard anyone else tries, they can never be you. Feelings of insignificance come when we try to measure up to or mimic someone else. Free yourself from the need to be like anyone else. Free yourself to be yourself.

This is so key. Don't miss this. The Church has had its identity stolen away, and with the loss of identity goes also the Church's power. This concept of Fatherhood is the reason we are instructed by Christ to always pray "IN THE NAME OF THE LORD JESUS". Now, prayer in the Name of Jesus is not a hocus-pocus statement to be thrown on the end of a prayer at the dinner table signaling to us that it's okay to eat. No, no. "In the Name of JESUS" is a statement of acknowledgement of authority. When you use the Name of Jesus, you're telling the enemy, the sickness, the spirit of poverty, of disease, of addiction and the very atmosphere itself that you understand who your Daddy is! Come on somebody! That's shouting material. I'm praying right now as you're reading this, that the Holy Spirit will begin to reveal to you that you have power in the Name of your Father through the blood of Jesus over every sickness, disease or circumstance in your life. Speak the Word in the authority of your Father, and every chain will be broken. Speak the Word, and every mountain has to move.

We get so caught up in the Word itself. The Word is so very important, but more than the Word, it's WHOSE Word it is that makes all the difference in the world. For instance, let's say a passerby tells you your blood pressure is high. Well, most likely you wouldn't think a thing about it because, after all, who are they to say such a thing. They're no doctor. They're just some person you passed on the street. But, if your doctor tells you your blood pressure is high, you will have a totally different reaction. The word is the same. It's the same bit of information; however, the person giving the word has authority to validate the word. We can find an example of this in the Bible:

Acts chapter 19 and verses 13-16

(13.) Some Jews who went around driving out evil spirits tried to invoke the name of the Lord Jesus over those who were demon-possessed. They would say, "in the Name of Jesus, whom Paul preaches, I command you to come out."

(14.) Seven sons of Sceva, a Jewish chief priest, were doing this.

(15.) One day an evil spirit answered them, "Jesus I know, and I know about Paul, but who are you?"

(16.) Then the man with the evil spirit jumped on them and overpowered them all. He gave them such a beating that they ran out of the house naked and bleeding.

(NIV)

These Jewish men were speaking the Word. The Word was the very Word of God. But they had no sense of sonship. They didn't understand who their Father was. They didn't know Him, and because they didn't know their Father, they didn't know their identity. Identity is crucial. Identity is the basis of the Kingdom of God. Identity is the basis of the Bible. The world was created for the sons of God. In the next chapter, we will study seven keys that will help you discover your identity.

CHAPTER

DISCOVERING YOUR IDENTITY

For over six thousand years, man has walked this earth, and for the entirety of that time there has been an assault on the identity of a man. For all practical purposes I must note that each time I use the term *man* throughout this book I am speaking expressly about the human race or mankind in general. The "Identity Crisis" is the enemy's oldest tactic of deception. In the book of Genesis, in his first recorded interaction with man, the enemy beguiled Eve and then Adam by challenging their identity and causing the *sons* of God to question who they were. Lets take a look at Scripture.

Genesis chapter 3 and verses 4-5
(4.) And the (enemy in the form of a) *serpent said unto the woman, Ye shall not surely die.*

(5.) For God doth know that in the day ye eat thereof, then Your eyes shall be opened, and ye shall be as God, knowing good and evil.

(KJV, parenthetical notes mine)

We can see clearly here that this is an assault on Adam and Eve's identity. "Eat and you'll be like God." They were already like God. They resembled Him in every way. They bore His appearance, His wisdom and His features. They were made in His likeness; in His very reflection were they made.

The Word of God declares in the book of Genesis:

Genesis chapter 1 and verses 26-27
*(26.) And God said, let us make man in our **IMAGE**, after our **LIKENESS**: and let them have dominion over the fish of the sea, and over the fowl of the air, and over the cattle, and over all the earth, and over every creeping thing that creepeth upon the earth.*

*(27.) So God created **man in his own image, in the image of God created He Him**: male and female created He them.*

(KJV, emphasis mine)

In fact, Adam and Eve were created so much in the likeness or image of God that He gave them his authority to name, to rule over and to have absolute dominion over every thing on earth. You wouldn't give absolute rule to someone you think *might* be your son or daughter, nor would you let just anyone have the keys to your house or drive your car. No, before you would bestow the honor of authority, you would ensure you were absolutely certain that person was your son or your daughter. There are many good people on the earth. There are many talented people, many rich and powerful people. There are even many popular people, such as movie stars, performing artists, athletes and so on. But, none of them have or should have your blessing of authority. Only a son or daughter has that right. Adam and Eve had that right. They were made the literal *sons* of God. Adam and Eve were the apple of God's eye. They consumed His thoughts. They were the pinnacle of his joy. God loved them so much that He gave them His image. He gave them His ability and authority to govern all the earth.

Genesis chapter 2 and verses 19-20
(19.) And out of the ground the Lord God formed every beast of the field, and every fowl of the air; **and brought them unto Adam to see what he would call them: and whatsoever Adam called every living creature, that was the name thereof.**

(20.) **And Adam gave names to all** *cattle, and to the fowl of the air, and to every beast of the field, but for Adam there was not found an help meet for him.*

(KJV, emphasis mine)

So through the Word we see that there were none more like God than Adam and Eve. No other bore his name, no other had his authority, and no other was created after the likeness of God or in His Image. Adam was the absolute Son of God and Eve was the absolute daughter of God. Angels were not made in the image of God. They did not resemble Him. They did not have His authority. God did not walk with the angels in the cool of the day as he did with Adam and Eve (Genesis 3:8). Even Lucifer, the archangel, did not resemble God. We know him today as satan, the devil or our enemy. The book of Ezekiel describes in vivid detail the appearance of Lucifer the archangel, or satan as we now know him.

Ezekiel chapter 28 and verses 12-19
(12.) Son of man, take up a lamentation upon the king of Tyrus (satan), *and say unto him, thus saith the Lord God; Thou sealest up the sum, full of wisdom, and perfect in beauty.*

(13.) Thou hast been in Eden the garden of God; every precious stone was thy covering, the sardius, topaz and the diamond, the beryl, the onyx, and the jasper, the sapphire, the emerald, and the carbuncle, and the gold; the workmanship of thy tabrets and of thy pipes was prepared in the day that thou was created.

(14.) Thou art the anointed cherub that covereth; and I have set thee so: thou was upon the holy mountain of God; thou has walked up and down in the midst of the stones of fire.

(15.) Thou wast perfect in thy ways from the day that thou wast created, till iniquity was found in thee.

(16.) By the multitude of thy merchandise they have filled the midst of thee with violence, and thou hast sinned: therefore I will cast thee as profane out of the mountain of God: and I

will destroy thee, O covering cherub, from the midst of the stones of fire.

(17.) Thine heart was lifted up because of thy beauty, thou hast corrupted thy wisdom by reason of thy brightness: I will cast thee to the ground, I will lay thee before kings, that they may behold thee.

(18.) Thou has defiled thy sanctuaries by the multitude of thine iniquities, by the iniquity of thy traffic; therefore I will bring forth a fire from the midst of thee, it shall devour thee, and I will bring thee to ashes upon the earth in the sight of all them that behold thee.

(19.) All they that know thee among the people shall be astonished at thee: I will make thee a terror, and never shalt thou be any more.

(KJV)

Verse 15 is our key verse here. It is in this verse that we witness the creation of satan. Yes, he was created with amazing talents and beautiful coverings. But, that's just it. He was created, not *formed*. Man was formed in the image of God. Man was modeled after God almighty, after God Himself. Satan with all his abilities and coverings was not made in the image of God; therefore, satan could never have the authority of God. Satan was a created being. Man was a created son. Man was formed in God's likeness and, therefore, was made to bear the name of God. With the name of God comes the authority of God.

This is why we can consecrate ourselves unto God, believing His Word above all else, pray in the wonderful name of Jesus and know that demons have to flee. This is why we can believe and speak God's Word and immovable mountains have to move. We are the likeness of God. Through Christ's blood we can once again become covenant *sons*. God has given all authority in heaven and earth unto the Name, the Name of Jesus, but it doesn't stop there. God, through Jesus, extended the right hand of *sonship* to us. Now we can pray in the Name of Jesus, which signifies that we are in the royal lineage of God, and sickness has to leave our bodies. Disease has to dry up. Cancer has to die. Addictions are broken. Lives are set free. It's not by our ability that this happens. It's through God's authority. Satan wants that authority, but he will never have that authority because he was not created to be a son of God. Satan knows this, and since he cannot have the authority of God, his motive is to strip you of your authority. He does this by causing you to question who God made you to be.

Thus far, we've been working at this thing from the inside out. My goal is to uncover Satan's tactic of "Identity Crisis" in order to cause you to ask yourself this question: *'If Satan is after my identity, then WHO AM I? If the enemy's goal through sickness, through poverty, through pain and depression is to cause me to give up and stop short of the prize, then WHO AM I?'* Ask yourself this question: *'If the forces of hell are arrayed against me like this, WHO AM I?'* Then make aloud this declaration: *'I must be someone important. There must be something very important for me to do with my life and in my lifetime. There must be a "God assignment" for my life.'* You know the enemy doesn't send out the forces of hell for some mamsy-pamsy, weak, do-nothing person. No, stand up and realize that the reason you're fighting what you're fighting like your fighting it is because the enemy knows that if he's going to stop you, he's got to do it now before you realize who you are because of Who you belong to. There is a demonic attack against your life, not because the enemy hates you, but because God has favored you... because God has big plans for you... because God has a "God assignment" over your life.

God reveals your assignment here on Earth through dreams. When God wanted to reveal to Joseph what he was to do and who he was to become, He did it through a dream. Your assignment is always the key to discovering who God created you to be. Each person has a very specific assignment or roll to play in his or her lifetime. There is a calling, or "God assignment", over the life of each person walking the planet. Discover *what* you were created to do, and you'll discover *who* you were created to be.

In order to discover your identity, you must first discover your lineage. In other words, in order to discover *who* you are, you must first discover *Whose* you are. God doesn't create sub par anything. Everything God creates is packed with earth-changing power. To discover your identity, you must discover your God and Father. The Apostle Luke put it best in his Biblical book, "The ACTS of the Apostles".

Acts chapter 17 and verse 28
'For it is in Him (God) *we live and move and have our being.'*
As some of your own poets have said, 'we are His (God's)
offspring'.

(NIV)

Luke is saying that you cannot live or have your being outside of God. He goes on to say that we, mankind, are the offspring of God. If you are the offspring of God, that means you are the son or daughter of God, and since you are the son or daughter of God, you are of extreme importance. Because you are the son or daughter of God, your identity lies within the role or assignment God has destined for you to fulfill. No father has a son or daughter without having hopes, dreams and plans for that child's life. God has a plan for your life. God designed you with a specific purpose in mind. You were made for a reason. Your assignment holds your identity, and likewise, your identity holds your assignment. Every father dreams of holding his child on his lap and recanting his stories of overcoming adverse circumstances and conquering seemingly hopeless situations. Every father desires to pass to his son or daughter the family history or lineage. The reason fathers desire this is because he knows that if the child can see what he's been able to accomplish, the child will find security in knowing that they can, at the very least, do the same. In other words, *'If daddy can do it, then so can I!'* Son or daughter of God, there is no mountain you cannot climb, no ocean you cannot cross, no giant you cannot slay. If God be for you, who can be against you? Through Christ, or, as the son of almighty God, I can do *all* things.

Discovering your identity is about intimacy with God your Father. Through time spent at His feet, you will discover all He has for you. The book of Jeremiah declares:

Jeremiah chapter 29 and verse 11
"For I know the plans I have for you," declares the Lord, "plans to prosper you and not to harm you, plans to give you hope and a future."

(NIV)

This revelation from God came to Jeremiah in a time of intimacy with Him. A time of separation. A holy time. God longs for each one of His *sons* to spend intimate time with Him. His heart's desire is that you would walk with Him in the cool of the day as Adam and Eve did. God is longing for fellowship with you.

Revelation chapter 3 and verse 20
Here I am! I stand at the door and knock. If anyone hears my voice and opens the door, I will come in and eat with him, and he with Me.

(NIV)

God is knocking on the doors of the hearts of men and women, desiring to come in and have intimate conversation, intimate fellowship and intimate communion. Your identity is found in the Father. The more time you spend with the Father, the more your identity will become evident. The more time you spend in His Word, the more you will know what you were created to do and who you were created to be. I want to challenge you to consecrate a special portion of your day each morning and each evening to God. This is the key to "Discovering Your Identity".

KNOWING IS POWER

If you were asked to identify yourself, you would probably pull out some form of "ID". There is bound to be something you carry with you that describes or identifies you. People most often carry some type of identification that entails a physical description and most likely a relational description to an organization or another person. You might have a driver's license, an employee badge, a debit or credit card, a library card, a union card, military dog tags or a law enforcement officer's badge. These are just a few of the many types of IDs commonly carried today. The people to whom these identification cards belong carry them with them literally everywhere they go, foreign or domestic. I carry many forms of identification with me every day. While some IDs are only carried on special occasions or under specific circumstances (i.e., a passport or visa), every person according to United States law must have some form of valid identification.

One of the greatest fears people of our day contend with is that of losing identity. The term *identity theft* is a commonly discussed topic in today's society, and identity theft regularly appears as a major headline in today's media outlets. Credit card and security companies alike are making multiple billions of dollars per year offering protection against the theft of a person's identity. If someone acquires your sensitive personal information, they have the power to essentially become you, and with your identity follows access to your assets through access points like credit card information, bank account information, social security numbers and various passwords, just to name a few. If someone gains your personally identifying information, they could potentially take everything you own leaving your life in shambles, your credit irreversibly ruined and your financials bankrupted. Our personal identities are so important, so crucial in the natural that we guard them with our lives. Have you ever left a purse or wallet in a restaurant or store by accident? Do you recall the feeling of terror and desperation as you frantically call the place of business alerting them of the mistake while rushing back as quickly as possible? What were you fearful of? Your fear rested not only on the possibility of your cash and personal belongings being lost or stolen, but greater than that on your identity falling into the wrong hands. We often see adds on television or in print that urge us to establish safeguards against identity theft, and all of this, all of the worry, all of the measures of safeguarding your identity, are only to protect your *physical* identity. Why? Because identity is ever so important.

Identity Defines Your Purpose in Life

As important as our identity is in regard to finances and possessions, there is an even more important identity that is based on who we are and what we are, as opposed to what we physically own or do. Here is an analogy. When a man is asked to describe himself, he will typically respond by explaining what he does for a living. His response may be, "I'm an engineer," or, "I'm a doctor," or, "I'm a minister," and so on and so forth. This is nearly always the first identifying feature a man will bring up in the presence of another man. The initial questions men ask one another following an introduction or greeting will normally sound something like, "How are you? How's the business going? What are you into these days?" A woman, on the other hand, often identifies herself by her relationships to other people. "I'm a mother"; "I'm a daughter"; "I'm a friend of so and so." This is most often the predominant subject a woman will discuss with other women.

Without any malicious intent involved, these intangible identities can be broken, damaged or even lost. It happens when a child leaves home and that mother's primary title is no longer "Mom" or when a husband passes away and she's no longer "So and So's wife." A man often experiences the effects of identity loss after he is laid off from a treasured job or retires from his career. When these changes in life occur, whether expected or unexpected, that man will no longer be recognized as the engineer he once was or the carpenter, minister or doctor everyone knew him to be. Physical relationships and occupations often become physical identities, and these identities then become the very purpose of our lives. Their loss can translate into having no reason to continue living.

Have you ever known or observed an older person doing incredibly well, getting up each morning and continuing on in his or her career or in managing a business long after the age of retirement? That individual, whether man or woman, can be doing so well, be in good health and remain very sharp mentally. Then for some reason they are no longer working, perhaps due to physical restrictions or to their employer forcing them to retire. Now that person who, despite his or her age, seemingly had the world by the tail, suddenly and very rapidly begins to decline in health and oftentimes passes on shortly after their identity is lost. Is it because their health suddenly took a turn for the worse? Or did their health take a turn for the worse because they lost their identity?

So, now we have established that we all have a physical identity. We have also looked at how we convey that identity through various forms of description or *ID* and how we associate who we are with our occupation or relationships with others. However, as a redeemed covenant-being, you and I have a much higher and much more important identity. When you receive the precious blood of Jesus and declare Him to be your Savior, you are redeemed from your sin, and instantaneously you come into right standing with God your Father. You are, in a sense, like the prodigal son returning to right relationship with your Father and Creator, God.

Colossians chapter 2 and verses 9-10
(9.) **For in Christ all the fullness of the Deity** *lives in bodily form.*

(10.) **And you have been given the fullness in Christ**, *who is the head over every power and authority.*

(NIV, emphasis mine)

Too many "Christians" receive Christ and amend their lifestyles, which is wonderful and to be expected, but never change their view or internal picture of themselves. And it is because of this wrong, distorted or often missing internal picture that we remain powerless, puny, poverty-stricken, sick and often relatively in the same mental, physical, relational and financial state as people in the world. You cannot receive your God-given inheritance until you come to the realization of who you are in Christ. Your mental picture of who you are must change in order for you to receive all that God has in store for you. The difference between a sick son of God and a healed son of God is nothing more than their understanding of God and their status as His heir. A person's understanding of God and their status as a son of God stems from their knowledge of the Word or promised covenant with God and their internal perception of themselves. God calls you a son in His word. The Word declares that you are a *co-heir* with or brother to Christ Himself. Let me prove it to you.

Luke chapter 3 and verse 38
... which was the son of Enos, which was the son of Seth, which was the son of Adam, which was the son of God.

(KJV)

In this very powerful verse of Scripture, the Word reveals and confirms that Adam was in fact the son of God. So, we all were created as *sons* of God, but because of sin, mankind was separated from God. We were each removed from our status as a son of God. Therefore, God, in order to redeem us from the curse of separation through sin, came to earth, robed himself in humanity and freely shed His perfect, sinless blood that you and I might once again be named a son of God. He, finding no other being worthy, offered himself, the spotless lamb, as propitiation for our sins.

Understanding this fact is a most important key. The book of Genesis explains that in the beginning we (man) were formed as the sons of God, and we have already discovered in chapters two and three of this book, *Identity Crisis* and *Discovering Your Identity*, Satan is a *created* being, not a *formed* son. Because of this, he could never receive the authority of God; therefore, Satan tried to take the authority of God and was removed from heaven (Isaiah 14:12; Luke 10:18). Satan, jealous of man's sonship status with God, tempted man. It was through man's giving in to this temptation that sin entered into mankind. Because of sin, the Holy and Just God, our Heavenly Father, rejected or separated Himself from His children, no longer calling us His sons but simply *man* alone. However, God so loved His offspring, and having found none other worthy, offered Himself. God offered His own blood as a sacrifice, forever buying back man from the curse of sin and once again bringing man into a covenant relationship with God as the *sons* of God. Wow, that's a mouthful, but if you open your spirit to receive the revelation of the sonship of God as described above, your life will never be the same.

You are a son of God. You're not an accident. You're not just here to be a father or a mother. You're not here to work 9:00-5:00 for forty years then retire and spend your days on a beach or on some golf course. You are a son or daughter of the Most High God. You were created to bring heaven to earth. You were created to cause the earth to resemble heaven through the Father's instruction. The Father's instruction is meant to be passed to you through time spent in fellowship with Him. As a son or daughter of God, you have power over every sickness and disease in existence. As a son or daughter of God, you have power over life and death. As a son or daughter of God, you have power over kings and rulers. As a son or daughter of God, you have power to bless and to curse. As a son or daughter of God, you have the authority *of* God. As a son or daughter of God, you have authority over *all* the power of the enemy.

This is the generation that will be partakers in the *Inferno Experience* with God. The generation that lives the *Inferno Experience* will understand their rightful authority as a son of God and use the enemy's power against him. I believe this is the generation that will stand in the face of the adversary regardless of what form he appears in and declare, *"No matter what, I will not bow to your system, satan."* This generation will rise up in power to destroy the works of the enemy. This *is* the generation that will know *who* they are because of *Whose* they are. When this revelation knowledge enters their hearts, they will stand up and bring forth a clarion call to arms against the kingdom of darkness. I believe we are on the precipice of the greatest revival, the greatest outpouring of the Holy Spirit this world has ever experienced. The greatest miracles, signs and wonders currently lie waiting within the bellies of this generation.

I believe this is the generation Joel prophesied about:

Joel chapter 2 and verses 28-32
(28.) "And afterward, I will pour out my Spirit on all people. And your sons and daughters will prophesy, your old men will dream dreams, your young men will see visions.

(29.) Even upon my servants, both men and women, I will pour out my Spirit in those days.

(30.) I will show wonders in the heavens and on earth, blood and fire and billows of smoke.

(31.) Then the sun will be turned to darkness and the moon to blood before the coming of the great and dreadful day of the LORD.

(32.) And everyone who calls on the name of the Lord will be saved; for on Mount Zion and in Jerusalem there will be **deliverance***, as the Lord has said, even among the survivors whom the Lord calls.*

(NIV, emphasis mine)

If you're alive and breathing on the earth today, you are a part of this generation: God's generation. No matter your age, race or social status, God has selected you to be a part of His time-of-the-end generation. You are a demon-chasing, hell-razing, mountain-moving child of God. There is greatness on you, in you, and greatness will come through you. Lay aside every excuse, every doubt and every weight that may be stopping you. Rise up in power because you *are* a son or daughter of Almighty God. The power is in knowing, and "Knowing is Power."

The city of Babylon

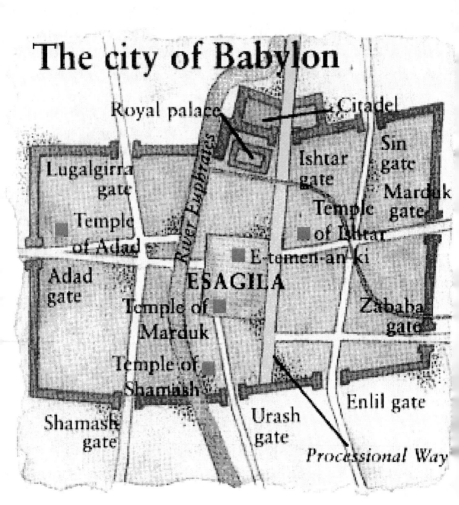

Royal palace — Citadel

Lugalgirra gate

Sin gate

Ishtar gate

Marduk gate

Temple of Adad

River Euphrates

Temple of Ishtar

E-temen-an-ki

Adad gate

ESAGILA

Temple of Marduk

Zababa gate

Temple of Shamash

Shamash gate

Urash gate

Enlil gate

Processional Way

EXPERIENCING THE FIRE

Let's take a moment to explore, to journey into the lives and character of Belteshazzar, Shadrach, Meshach and Abednego, or Daniel and "the three Hebrew boys" as we know them. Many people heard the Bible stories, *The Three Hebrew Boys* and *Daniel and the Lion's Den,* as they were told to them in children's church or by their parents growing up. When raised in church and around such amazing stories as those told in Daniel chapter 3, we tend to think of such stories as well, larger-than-life so to speak. Such stories are so far removed from our way of life in America and in the American church that oftentimes it may be all but impossible to relate to such stories or examples. Their contexts are so foreign and often so crude that we begin to immortalize the men and women of which these stories tell, placing them somehow above us in valor, intellect or even genetics. Many times we ***classify*** these historical figures as if to say that they belong to a certain group or class of "greater" people, deducing this and forming that classification because such people were prophets or kings or because they were among the disciples or rulers of their day. We think these "greater" people somehow had an innate ability that we as common or normal people in today's time simply do not have. I hope over the course of the next few minutes to take you through a brief overview of Daniel, Shadrach, Meshach and Abednego in order to debunk some of the "larger-than-life-isms" that you may have, ultimately unveiling the true source of ability or strength behind such great men. Let's find out what the Bible has to say about these men of God.

Daniel chapter 1 and verses 1-7
(1.) In the third year of the reign of Jehoiakim king of Judah, Nebuchadnezzar king of Babylon came to Jerusalem and besieged it.

(2.) And the Lord gave Jehoiakim king of Judah into his hand, along with part of the vessels of the house of God; and he carried them into the land of Shinar (Babylon) to the house of his god and placed the vessels in the treasury of his god.

(3.) And the (Babylonian) king told Ashpenaz, the master of his eunuchs, to bring in some of the children of Israel, both of the royal family and of the nobility,

(4.) Youths without blemish, well-favored in appearance and skillful in all wisdom, discernment, and understanding, apt in learning knowledge, competent to stand and serve in the king's palace and to teach them the literature and language of the Chaldeans.

(5.) And the king assigned for them daily portions of his own rich and dainty food and of the wine which he drank. They were to be so educated and so nourished for three years that at the end of that time they might stand before the king.

(6.) Among these were of the children of Judah: Daniel, Hananiah, Mishael, and Azariah.

(7.) The chief of the eunuchs gave them names: Daniel he called Belteshazzar (the king's attendant), Hananiah he called Shadrach, Mishael he called Meshach, and Azariah he called Abednego.

(AMP)

As recorded in the Book of Daniel, these men - Daniel and the three Hebrew boys - were taken captive with numerous other men from Jerusalem. In the writings of Josephus, a well-known Jewish historian, we find an exact number concerning the sum of people taken with Daniel and the three Hebrew boys for the king's service. Josephus records in his book entitled, *The Antiquities of the Jews*, along about the eighth or ninth division, that the total number of skilled, beautiful, gifted, wise and valiant men, strong both in spirit and in body, who were taken with Daniel and his cohort was in excess of ten thousand. Think about that for a moment. More than ten thousand men were equally skilled, equally beautiful, equally as handy, both in body and in mind. Daniel and the three Hebrew boys were just one of the many. They were seemingly just a face in the crowd.

Have you ever been there? Having had God speak to you about your future, about your destiny only to find out that there are at least ten thousand other men or women just like you, maybe even some better who have the same calling. There is a time in every child of God's life that God exposes you to this reality that there are so many others that are capable and skilled, many others with the right style and vision. It's in that moment that many ministers, many praise and worship leaders, many chosen people of God, give up on, or place on hold the purpose of God for their lives. Seeing the great number of capable men and women surrounding them, Daniel, Hananiah, Mishael, and Azariah didn't shrink from the vision of God for their lives. They didn't back up or place on hold the dreams and plans God had for them. They didn't say, *'Well, it was a good idea, but it doesn't look like we're going make it.'* They weren't intimidated. They didn't just try to get by and hope something happened. No! They soared into the spotlight. They blazed a trail strait to the top and with record speed. In less than the three years the King of Babylon had previously set aside, Daniel and the three Hebrew boys had grown in wisdom above even the king's elders and chief advisors, placing them at the pinnacle of leadership of the nation of Babylon.

How did they do it? How did Daniel, Hananiah, Mishael and Azariah, four men among a sea of more than ten thousand others, many of which were more capable, seemingly out of nowhere in less than two years rise to the level at which we find them in the Book of Daniel? The answer to this question is so profound yet so simple that many pass right over it, failing to see with the eyes of the Spirit. Many are so intimidated with what they see in the natural, they fail to see what is happening in the Spirit. Before we get to the answer behind the unusual ability of the three Hebrew men and their companion Daniel, we must discuss a very important law of God:

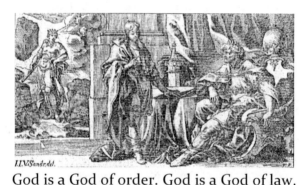

God is a God of order. God is a God of law.
He is a God of principle.
God is a God of promise and of principle. His promises
will never violate His principles, and His
principles will never cancel or
negate His promises.

Before anything manifests in the natural, it must first manifest in the spiritual. This is God's Law, His order. Man

75

is living in two worlds at the same time: The natural world, and the spiritual world, both of which are very real, both of which are very tangible. The Law of God is that the spiritual governs the natural. The spirit world must conceive and make manifest before the natural world can conceive and make manifest. This law is found over and over again in the Bible, beginning in the book of Genesis.

Genesis chapter 1 and verses 1-5
(1.) In the beginning God created the heavens and the earth.

(2.) Now the earth was (or became) *formless and empty, darkness was over the surface of the deep,* **and the Spirit of God was hovering over the waters.**

(3.) **And God said**, *"Let there be light," and there was light.*

(4.) God saw that the light was good, and he separated the light from the darkness.

(5.) **God called** *the light "day" and the darkness* **he called** *"night." And there was evening, and there was morning—the first day.*

(NIV, parenthetical notes mine)

St. John chapter 1 and verses 1-5 and 14
(1.) In the beginning was the Word, and the Word was with God, and the Word was God.

(2.) The same (The Word) was in the beginning with God.

(3.) Through him all things were made; and without Him was nothing made that has been made.

*(4.) **In Him was life, and that life was the light of men.***

(5.) The light shines in the darkness, but darkness has not understood it.

(14.) The Word became flesh and made his dwelling among us. We have seen his Glory, the Glory of the One and Only, who came from the Father, full of grace and truth.

(NIV)

St. John chapter 4 verse 24
God is a Spirit: and they that worship Him must worship Him in spirit (the Holy Ghost) *and in truth* (the Word of God).

(KJV)

In the beginning there was nothing but God -- God alone, standing on the corner of nowhere, beside nothing, just God. God all by himself. And God who is a Spirit, who lives in a spirit world, surrounded by spirit things, spoke. Now since God was first and before Him there was none or no thing, and since it is by God and God alone that the world and all that is in it exist, we must conclude that before the natural there was the spiritual, and therefore, before the natural can ever be there must first be the spiritual. Before Job could experience the attack of the enemy, God – who is Spirit – released the enemy to attack him. Before Mary, the mother of Jesus, could birth the Messiah into this world, she first was told in a visitation from the Spirit of God. So God's law is, "First the spiritual, then the natural". Nothing happens on earth until it first is conceived in the heavens.

Daniel, Hananiah, Mishael and Azariah knew this law of God. They knew that it was never the Jewish intellect, the Jewish power, or the Jewish good looks that brought them from the land of Egypt. Daniel, Hananiah, Mishael and Azariah knew it was not the power of Moses that parted the Red Sea or the might of king David that slew Goliath. They knew that the distinguishing factor would not be might or power or valor or the fairness of their outward appearance. These men knew that it wouldn't be through their "inner-kingdom" connections that they would fulfill all that God had promised. No my friend. Daniel, Hananiah, Mishael and Azariah knew that if they were to fulfill all that God had spoken they must rely on the power of a Holy God, the power of the Holy Spirit. That why immediately, as soon we see Daniel and the three Hebrew boys brought into the king's training, they make a covenant with God concerning their future. They decide that no meat will enter their mouth all the remaining days of their lives. Also, neither shall any sweet thing or pleasant drink enter their body. They will be set apart for God's use all the days of their lives. They make this covenant before God and each other and then display their trust in the God they serve by putting their covenant to the test.

Daniel chapter 1 and verses 8-20
(8.) But Daniel resolved not to defile himself with the royal food and wine, and he asked the chief official for permission not to defile himself this way.

(9.) Now God had caused the official to show favor and sympathy to Daniel,

(10.) but the official told Daniel, "I am afraid of my lord the king, who has assigned your food and drink. Why should he see you looking worse than the other young men your age? The king would then have my head because of you."

(11.) Daniel then said to the guard whom the chief official had appointed over Daniel, Hananiah, Mishael and Azariah,

(12.) "Please test you servants for ten days: Give us nothing but vegetables to eat and water to drink.

(13.) Then compare our appearance with that of the young men who eat the royal food, and treat your servants in accordance with what you see."

(14.) So he agreed to this and tested them for ten days.

(15.) At the end of the ten days they looked healthier and better nourished than any of the young men who ate the royal food.

(16.) So the guard took away their choice food and the wine they were to drink and gave them vegetables instead.

(17.) To these four young men God gave knowledge and understanding of all kinds of literature and learning. And Daniel could understand visions and dreams of all kinds.

(18.) At the end of the time set by the king to bring them in, the chief official presented them to Nebuchadnezzar.

(19.) The king talked with them and found none equal to Daniel, Hananiah, Mishael and Azariah; so they entered the king's service.

(20.) In every matter of wisdom and understanding about which the king questioned them, he found them ten times better than all the magicians and enchanters in his whole kingdom.

(NIV)

I believe today we are living in times more similar to that of Daniel, Hananiah, Mishael and Azariah than ever before. This is the generation that will rise up in power through Nazarite consecration and shake the world like never before. There are so many things contained within the scriptures listed above, so many types and shadows that parallel our Christian lives today. Your consecration to God will be the difference in your life. When you align yourself with the will of the Father, abandoning all else to seek His face and to see His will on Earth, amazing things begin to transpire. There is no God like our God: no God that is able to heal, able to fill, able to save, able to rescue to the uttermost. He is a God that always answers by fire, a God whose arms are not short that He cannot reach, nor His ears dull that He cannot hear. If you had the option to rely on either a limitless God who is able to do anything exceedingly and abundantly above anything that we could even imagine, or the power that you possess as a mere man or woman, what would be your choice? Too many people are relying on their power or their abilities. Too many men and women of God are relying on their talent or personality to make a difference for Christ in this world. Too many pastors, preachers and praise and worship leaders who made their start in the power of prayer are now trying to continue in the pizzazz of personality. We must like never before rely on the sovereign power of a limitless God.

Many people, especially men and women of God, are almost at arms concerning the government and the state of the world. Doom and gloom are not in short supply. Dare I make this statement? The Church does not answer to the government, but the government must answer to true apostolic men and women of God. We have power over every authority of the enemy. God is not coming again for a weak-wristed Church full of people with something  bad to say about the current office holders. King Nebuchadnezzar was a pagan. He was a man that didn't even believe in God, a man that sacrificed to idols and cast children into the fires of idol gods, but with one purpose and four words, three men shaped a nation and changed a generation. Their purpose was consecration unto God, to be set apart as Holy unto the Lord expressly for His pleasure and purpose. Their words: I WIL NOT BOW. I won't bow to the idols of this world. I won't bow to the lust of the flesh, the pride of life or the lust of the eye. I won't bend to the systems of this world. And the men were Hananiah, Mishael and Azariah, "the three Hebrew boys".

Neither time nor the confines of this chapter will allow us to continue to expound on the lives of Daniel, Hananiah, Mishael and Azariah. However, I must inform you that you are the Daniel Generation. You are the generation that will not only dream dreams and see visions, but those who choose to consecrate themselves as holy unto the Lord will be given the ability to understand and interpret the events of the day in which we live. Nations will be shaped. Generations will be changed based upon the Word of God within you. Your life is filled with the purpose of God. This is the greatest hour to be alive. The very best is yet to come. The *secret* behind the success of Daniel, Hananiah, Mishael and Azariah was their ability to rely on the ability of God through their personal consecration.

THE FELLOWSHIP
OF THE FIRE

The Fire of God is a term used often in the Bible and throughout Christianity as a whole. It is also the focal point of this book and the reason for my writing. *Fire* or *the Fire of God* as a term is used in the Bible over 370 times. *The Fire of God* is found in both the Old and New Testaments with great regularity. *The Fire of God* is a term often used in prophecy, protection and confirmation of a covenant. In the Old Testament, Moses' calling to become the deliverer was confirmed with a burning bush. Also in the Old Testament, a pillar of fire was the leading, guiding, protecting visual sign or demonstration of the presence of God with the people of Israel as they journeyed through the wilderness. Christ was prophesied about in Isaiah saying, *"Behold, He, The Christ, will come and baptize you with the Spirit of God, and with Fire."*

Isaiah chapter 4 and verse 4
The Lord will wash away the filth from beautiful Zion; and cleanse Jerusalem of its bloodstains by the spirit of judgment (the Holy Spirit) *and the spirit of fire.*

(NIV)

This scripture is foretelling of the Messiah coming to Earth to wash away the sins of the world through His blood on the cross and a foretelling of the introduction of the baptism of the Holy Ghost and the Fire of God. The revelation of prophecy contained in the scriptures written by the prophet Isaiah is again retold and yet still foretold by the cousin of Christ and prophet in his own right, John the Baptist.

John the Baptist, standing on the muddy banks of the Jordan River miles removed from civilization, is preaching, prophesying and baptizing in the wilderness. John is 765 years removed from the time of the prophecy of Isaiah when suddenly the Holy Spirit moves upon him, and he loudly proclaims these resounding words:

Luke chapter 3 and verse 16
John answered them all, "I baptize you with water. But one more powerful than I will come, the thongs of whose sandals I am not worthy to untie. He will baptize you with the Holy Spirit and fire."

(NIV)

Shortly thereafter comes the One prophesied about, The Christ, Jesus. He is baptized by John to fulfill prophesy and begins His ministry. Many great things, signs and wonders, did Jesus perform during his three and one third years of public ministry, so many things that the Bible records that all the books in the world could not hold the writings depicting the acts and teachings of Christ. Jesus Christ fulfilled His public ministry on the cross, forever washing away the sins of mankind for all that will receive Him. Glory!

Christ is then three days in the grave, during which time he defeats Satan forever, victoriously taking back the keys to the Kingdom of God. The Messiah then rises again from the grave and gives his disciples this final instruction, *"Go and tarry in Jerusalem until you be endued with Power from on High."*

Luke chapter 24 and verses 49-51
(49.) "And, behold, I send the promise of my father on you: but tarry you in the city of Jerusalem, until you be clothed with power from on high."

(50.) And then He led them out as far as Bethany, and He lifted up His hands, and blessed them.

(51.) And it came to pass, while he blessed them, he was parted from them, and carried up into heaven.

(KJV 2000)

The power of which Christ is speaking is the Holy Ghost and Fire of God. Think about this for a moment. All of humanity for more than four thousand years is waiting in anticipation for the coming of the Promised One, The Messiah. Contained within every book of the Bible and every Jewish writing throughout the ages is some type of promise and prediction concerning the coming of Christ. The types and shadows of the Hebrew Bible concerning the Messiah are too numerous to count. Even all of time was in waiting for this moment. The world itself was anticipating His arrival. So the Messiah, the Promised One, Jesus having fulfilled the will of the Father and completed His public ministry leaves the world with this statement, *"Go and wait for the Fire."* He could have said anything. He could have prophesied the antichrist or the exact year of the end of days. If it were me, I would have said some deeply spiritual statement that contained within itself the answers to all the mysteries of the world. But Christ, Emmanuel, God with us, says these simple words, *"Go wait for the Fire."*

Don't go left. Don't go right. Don't back up. Don't go forward. Don't form a committee; don't heal the sick; don't go home and rest. Don't even eat or drink. *Go wait for the Fire.* Go. Wait. For. The. Fire. Therefore, if the Fire of God is used throughout the Old and New Testament with regularity, and Christ's last command before his ascension into Heaven was concerning the necessity of the Fire of God in our lives, we must yet go deeper into this term, *the Fire of God*, to discover all it still holds for us.

The word *fire* in the Hebrew is *'esh.* The Hebrew word *'esh* has many definitions, including, *Holy Fire, the Alter Fire, God's anger and the Supernatural Fire of God.* The last definition of the Hebrew word *'esh* is the one I want to focus on for the next while. That being; *'Esh- The Supernatural Fire of God.*

86

Throughout the Bible, the Supernatural Fire of God is related to the guiding, correcting, directing, protecting and purging forces of God. The previous definition for the Hebrew word *'esh*, meaning supernatural fire of God, is closely related to the Greek term, *theophany*. In the next section of this chapter, we will go deep into the meaning of the related term *theophany* and unveil the revelation concerning the final words of Christ, *"Go wait for the Fire."*

Theophany: from the Ancient Greek (ἡ) θεοφάνεια (*theophaneia*, meaning "the appearance of God"). This term refers to the appearance of God to a human or other being or to a divine disclosure.

The term *theophany* refers to the manifestation of God to man, the clear, understandable sign by which the presence of God is revealed. A number of *theophanies* are found in the Hebrew Bible, or Old Testament.

Now here are some examples of men and women of God from the scriptures receiving a visitation from God, or a *theophany*. The original Biblical terms behind the forming of the word *theophany* was a compilation of four Hebrew words including, *mar'eh* meaning "sight", and *mahazeh*, *hazon* or *hizzayon* all of which can be defined as "vision". The Bible states that God revealed Himself to man. God speaks with Adam and Eve in Eden;

Genesis chapter 3 and verses 9-19
(9.) But the Lord God called to the man, "Where are you?"

(10.) He answered, "I heard you in the garden, and I was afraid because I was naked; so I hid."

(11.) And he said, "Who told you that you were naked? Have you eaten from the tree that I commanded you not to eat from?"

(12.) The man said, "The woman you put here with me – she gave me some fruit from the tree, and I ate."

(13.) Then the Lord God said to the woman, "What is this you have done?"
The woman said, "The serpent deceived me, and I ate."

(14.) So the Lord God said to the serpent, "Because you have done this, Cursed are you above all livestock and all wild animals! You will crawl on your belly and you will eat dust all the days of your life.

(15.) And I will put enmity between you and the woman, and between your offspring and hers; he will crush your head, and you will strike his heal."

(16.) To the woman he said, "I will make your pains in childbearing very severe; with painful labor you will give birth to children. Your desire will be for your husband, and he will rule over you."

(17.) To Adam he said, "Because you listened to your wife and ate from the tree about which I commanded you, 'You must not eat from it,' "Cursed is the ground because of you;

through painful toil you will eat food from it all the days of your life.

(18.) It will produce thorns and thistles for you; and you will eat the plants of the field.

(19.) By the sweat of your brow you will eat your food until you return to the ground, since from it you were taken; for dust you are and to dust you will return."

(NIV)

. with Cain;

Genesis chapter 4 and verses 6-12
(6.) Then the Lord said to Cain, "Why are you angry? Why is your face downcast?

(7.) If you do what is right, will you not be accepted? But if you do not do what is right, sin is crouching at your door; it desires to have you, but you must rule over it."

(8.) Now Cain said to his brother Abel, "Let's go out to the field." While they were in the field, Cain attacked his brother Abel and killed him.

(9.) Then the Lord said to Cain, "Where is your brother Abel?" "I don't know," he replied. "Am I my brother's keeper?"

(10.) The Lord said, "What have you done? Listen! Your brother's blood cries out to me from the ground.

(11.) Now you are under a curse and driven from the ground,

which opened its mouth to receive your brother's blood from your hand.

(12.) When you work the ground, it will no longer yield its crops for you. You will be a restless wanderer on the earth."

(NIV)

with Noah;

Genesis chapter 9 and verses 9-15
(9.) "I now establish my covenant with you and with your descendants after you

(10.) and with every living creature that was with you – the birds, the livestock and all the wild animals, all those that came out of the ark with you – every living creature on earth.

(11.) I establish my covenant with you: Never again will all life be destroyed by the waters of a flood; never again will there be a flood to destroy the earth."

(12.) And God said, "This is a sign of the covenant I am making between me and you and every living creature with you, a covenant for all generations to come:

(13.) I have set my rainbow in the clouds, and it will be the sign of the covenant between me and the earth.

(14.) Whenever I bring clouds over the earth and the rainbow appears in the clouds,

(15.) I will remember my covenant between me and you and all living creatures of every kind. Never again will the waters become a flood to destroy all life.

Genesis chapter 6 and verse 13
So God said to Noah, "I am going to put an end to all people for the earth is filled with violence because of them. I am surely going to destroy both them and the earth.

Genesis chapter 7 and verse 1
The Lord then said to Noah, "Go in to the ark, you and your whole family, because I have found you righteous in this generation.

Genesis chapter 8 and verses 15-17
(15.) Then God said to Noah,

(16.) "Come out of the ark, you and your wife and your sons and their wives.

(17.) Bring out every kind of living creature that is with you – the birds the animals, and all the creatures that move along the ground – so they can multiply on the earth and be fruitful and increase in number on it."

(NIV)

with Noah's sons;

Genesis chapter 9 and verses 1
(1.) Then God blessed Noah and his sons, saying to them, "Be fruitful and increase in number and fill the earth."

(NIV)

and with Abraham;

Genesis chapter 17 and verses 1-8
(1.) When Abram was ninety-nine years old, the Lord appeared to him and said, "I am God Almighty; walk before me faithfully and be blameless.

(2.) Then I will make my covenant between me and you and will greatly increase your numbers."

(3.) Abram fell facedown, and God said to him,

(4.) "As for me, this is my covenant with you: You will be the father of many nations.

(5.) No longer will you be called Abram; your name will be Abraham, for I have made you a father of many nations.

(6.) I will make you very fruitful; I will make nations of you, and kings will come from you.

(7.) I will establish my covenant as an everlasting covenant between me and you and your descendants after you for the generations to come, to be your God and the God of your descendants after you.

(8.) The whole land of Canaan, where you now reside as a foreigner, I will give as an everlasting possession to you and your descendants after you; and I will be their God."

(NIV)

The first revelation that Moses had of God at the burning bush was *"a great sight"*; *"he was afraid to look"* at Him (Exodus 3:3,6). Samuel's dream is called *"the vision"*; afterward God was frequently *"seen"* at Shiloh (I Samuel 3:15,21). Isaiah's first revelation was also a sight of God.

Isaiah chapter 6 and verses 1-5
(1.) In the year that King Uzziah died, I saw the Lord, high and exalted, seated on a throne; and the train of his robe filled the temple.

(2.) Above him were seraphim, each with six wings: With two wings they covered their faces, with two they covered their feet, and with two they were flying.

(3.) And they were calling to one another:

*"Holy, holy, holy is the Lord Almighty;
the whole earth is full of his glory."*

(4.) At the sound of their voices the doorposts and thresholds shook and the temple was filled with smoke

(5.) "Woe to me!" I cried. "I am ruined! For I am a man of unclean lips, and I live among a people of unclean lips, and my eyes have seen the King, the Lord Almighty."

(NIV)

Amos had his visions (Amos 7:1,4; 8:1; 9:1), and so with Jeremiah (Jeremiah 1:11,13), Ezekiel (Ezekiel 1:1; 8:1-3), and Zechariah (Zecharaih 1:7), and, in fact, with all "seers," as they called themselves.

Balaam referred to himself as the one who had seen "the vision of the Almighty" (Numbers 24:4). Let's look closely at Eliphaz's account of his revelation of God:

Job chapter 4 and verses 13-16
(13.) "In thoughts from the vision of the night, when deep sleep falleth on men,

(14.) fear came upon me, and trembling, which made all my bones shake.

(15.) Then a spirit passed before my face; the hair of my flesh stood up.

(16.) It stood still, but I could not discern the form thereof; an image was before mine eyes, there was silence, and I heard a voice, saying..."

(KJV)

In the first five books of the Bible, known as the Torah, God spoke with his prophets in dreams and visions. However, He spoke with Moses *"mouth to mouth"*, *"as a man would speak with his neighbor,"* in clear sight and not in riddles (Numbers 12:6-8; Exodus 33:11; Deuteronomy 34:10).

The Burning Bush

While Moses was in Midian keeping the flock of Jethro his father-in-law, the angel of the Lord appeared to him in a flame of fire out of the midst of a bush that burned but was not consumed:

Exodus chapter 3 and verses 1-2

(1.) Now Moses was tending the flock of Jethro his father-in-law, the priest of Midian, and he led the flock to the far side of the wilderness and came to Horeb, the mountain of God.

(2.) There the angel of the Lord appeared to him in flames of fire from within a bush. Moses saw that though the bush was on fire it did not burn up.

(NIV)

It was during this encounter with the angel of the Lord, that God commissioned Moses to speak with Pharaoh and demand freedom for the people of Israel. From within the burning bush, God revealed to Moses that he would be the very one to lead the Israelites out of bondage and into precious freedom.

Exodus chapter 3 and verses 3-12

(3.) So Moses thought, "I will go over and see this strange sight—why the bush does not burn up."

(4.) When the Lord saw that he had gone over to look, God called to him from within the bush, "Moses! Moses!"

And Moses said, "Here I am."

(5.) "Do not come any closer," God said. "Take off your sandals, for the place where you are standing is holy ground."

(6.) Then he said, "I am the God of your father, the God of

Abraham, the God of Isaac and the God of Jacob." At this, Moses hid his face, because he was afraid to look at God.

(7.) The Lord said, "I have indeed seen the misery of my people in Egypt. I have heard them crying out because of their slave drivers, and I am concerned about their suffering.

(8.) So I have come down to rescue them from the hand of the Egyptians and to bring them up out of that land into a good and spacious land, a land flowing with milk and honey—the home of the Canaanites, Hittites, Amorites, Perizzites, Hivites and Jebusites.

(9.) And now the cry of the Israelites has reached me, and I have seen the way the Egyptians are oppressing them.

(10.) So now, go. I am sending you to Pharaoh to bring my people the Israelites out of Egypt."

(11.) But Moses said to God, "Who am I that I should go to Pharaoh and bring the Israelites out of Egypt?"

(12.) And God said, "I will be with you. And this will be the sign to you that it is I who have sent you: When you have brought the people out of Egypt, you will worship God on this mountain."

(NIV)

The Pillar of Cloud by Day and Fire by Night

God makes His divine presence and protection known by leading the Israelites out of Egypt and through the desert, appearing as a pillar of cloud during the day and a pillar of Fire, The Fire of God, at night.

Exodus chapter 13 and verses 21-22
(21.) By day the Lord went ahead of them in a pillar of cloud to guide them on their way and by night in a pillar of fire to give them light, so that they could travel by day or night.

(22.) Neither the pillar of cloud by day nor the pillar of fire by night left its place in front of the people.

(NIV)

On Mount Sinai

A *theophany* at Mount Sinai occurs in Exodus chapter 19. God appears with thunder and lightning, intense flames reaching to the sky, the blasts of a trumpet, and billows of smoke as the mountain quakes. Out of the midst of the flame and the cloud, the voice of Almighty God reveals the Ten Commandments.

Exodus chapter 19 and verses 16-25
(16.) On the morning of the third day there was thunder and lightning, with a thick cloud over the mountain, and a very loud trumpet blast. Everyone in the camp trembled.

(17.) Then Moses led the people out of the camp to meet with God, and they stood at the foot of the mountain.

(18.) Mount Sinai was covered with smoke, because the Lord descended on it in fire. The smoke billowed up from it like smoke from a furnace, and the whole mountain trembled

violently.

(19.) As the sound of the trumpet grew louder and louder, Moses spoke and the voice of God answered him.

(20.) The Lord descended to the top of Mount Sinai and called Moses to the top of the mountain. So Moses went up

(21.) and the Lord said to him, "Go down and warn the people so they do not force their way through to see the Lord and many of them perish.

(22.) Even the priests, who approach the Lord, must consecrate themselves, or the Lord will break out against them.

(23.) Moses said to the Lord, "The people cannot come up Mount Sinai, because you yourself warned us, 'Put limits around the mountain and set it apart as holy.'"

(24.) The Lord replied, "Go down and bring Aaron up with you. But the priests and the people must not force their way through to come up to the Lord, or he will break out against them."

(25.) So Moses went down to the people and told them.

(NIV)

God so desires to reveal Himself to His precious creation. It is his very nature to do so. We see this in Deuteronomy where the same account is given in similar fashion to the previous passage from Exodus.

Deuteronomy chapter 4 and verses 11,12, 33, & 36

(11.) You came near and stood at the foot of the mountain while it blazed with fire to the very heavens, with black clouds and deep darkness.

(12.) Then the Lord spoke to you out of the fire. You heard the sound of words but saw no form; there was only a voice.

...

(33.) Has any other people heard the voice of God speaking out of fire, as you have, and lived?

...

(36.) From heaven he made you hear his voice to discipline you. On earth he showed you his great fire, and you heard his words from out of the fire.

(NIV)

Moses in his blessing in Deuteronomy chapter 33 references this encounter as to the source of the election of Israel, except that he credits the point of departure for the *theophany* as Mount Sinai and not heaven. God appears on Sinai like a Holy Fire and comes *"accompanied by holy myriads"* (Deuteronomy 33:2).

In Isaiah and Ezekiel

Isaiah and Ezekiel received their great calling from God through *theophanies* in like fashion. Isaiah sees God on a high and lofty throne, lifted up amidst the praises of His people, His robe filling the temple of heaven. Before the throne stand the seraphim, the six-winged angels. With two wings they cover their faces so as not to gaze on God, for He is a Holy God, an all-consuming Fire, too white, pure and Holy for any to gaze upon. And with two wings they cover their feet, through modesty, and with the remaining two wings they fly. Their sole purpose is the everlasting praise of God as they cry, *"Holy, holy, holy is the Lord Almighty; the whole earth is full of his glory."* (Isaiah 6:3).

Ezekiel gives an even more grandiose account of an encounter with the great God of Israel. His throne appears as a wonderful chariot of Fire within a mighty storm, containing great clouds of ceaseless Fire and an unimaginable brightness. Out of the Fire, four cherubim emerge. They have the faces of men, each one has four wings, and the shape of their feet enables them to go to all four quarters of the earth quickly, seemingly effortlessly, without having to turn. (Ezekiel 10:20). Heavenly Fire, serving as torches, moves between them. The cherubim move together in complete harmony, venturing only where the Fire or Spirit of God leads them.

Beneath these creatures are wheels full of eyes. On their heads rests a firmament upon which is the throne of God. When the divine chariot moves, their wings rustle with a noise like thunder. On the throne, the prophet sees the Almighty in a form resembling that of a man. His body from the waist downward is shining like Fire (Ezekiel 8:2).

In the Psalms

The Psalmist David also experiences a *theophany,* seeing God in a similar fashion:

Psalm 18 and verses 8-16
(8.) Smoke rose from his nostrils;
consuming fire *came from his mouth,*
burning coals blazed *out of it.*

(9.) He parted the heavens and came down;
dark clouds were under his feet.

(10.) He mounted the cherubim and flew;
he soared on the wings of the wind.

(11.) He made darkness his covering, his canopy around him—
the dark rain clouds of the sky.

(12.) Out of the brightness of his presence clouds advanced,

with hailstones and bolts of lightning.

(13.) The Lord thundered from heaven;
the voice of the Most High resounded.

(14.) He shot his arrows and scattered the enemy,
with great bolts of lightning he routed them.

(15.) The valleys of the sea were exposed
and the foundations of the earth laid bare at your rebuke,
Lord, at the blast of breath from your nostrils.

(16.) He reached down from on high and took hold of me;
he drew me out of deep waters.

(NIV, emphasis mine)

Before God, the earth trembles and Fire glows. God rides on a cherub on the wings of the wind. God is surrounded with clouds that are outshone by His brightness, which resembles Fire. With thunder and lightning God destroys the enemies of the singer and rescues him.

So in short, a *theophany* is a Greek term for the appearance of God to man. In almost every appearance of God in the Bible, there is fire accompanying, surrounding or manifesting with or upon God Himself. God is a God of Fire, plain and simple. Fire has the same characteristics no matter where it is or what it's burning. Fire is unmistakable. When you see fire, you immediately know what it is. Fire is all-consuming. It burns everything in its path. Fire if presented with the right host becomes easily started, quickly spreading, and hard to contain. Fire is an equal-opportunity offender. Fire doesn't stop and regard your last name or personal connections before destroying your house or property. Fire leaves a recognizable path in its wake. No one is ever guessing. If anything has been burned with fire it's easily identified. Fire, when safely used, can warm a house and sterilize water and food. Fire serves two purposes: sterilization and illumination. Fire produces heat and light. When using fire to cook, in essence, through the process of controlled heat the food being prepared is sterilized or cooked. Fire produces light, which was used for thousands of years to help civilization see during the darkness of night. Whether through a candle, campfire or torch, fire emits light.

As it is in the natural, so it is in the spiritual. The fire of God comes to sterilize or sanctify as holy, consuming even the desire for sin. The Fire of God also comes to illuminate the path that we should take.

Acts chapter 13 and verses 2-3
(2.) While they (Paul and Barnabas) *were worshiping the Lord and fasting, the Holy Spirit said, "Set apart for me Barnabas and Saul for the work to which I have called them."*

(3.) So after they had fasted and prayed, they placed their hands on them and sent them off.

(NIV)

We see in this scripture Paul and Barnabas, through the illumination of the Holy Spirit, are set aside for the work of God unto the Gentiles. We are living in a day in which we need the illumination of the Holy Ghost like never before. If you fail in your assignment, it will only be because you did not spend enough time with the Holy Ghost and Fire. The Fire of God is meant to sanctify you and to illuminate the path God has chosen for you. Take the next thirty days and spend thirty minutes in the presence of God. Read aloud one chapter of Proverbs a day, beginning with proverbs one on day one and proverbs chapter thirty-one on the thirty-first day. Make sure to bring a note pad or journal and pen with you. The revelation or illumination of God that will come to you through the His Holy Spirit and Fire will change your life. You will never be the same.

If you've ever had to endure the sight of someone on fire, you will notice that it doesn't matter how old or young a person may be, they all act the same. If a person is on fire, demeanor, disposition and deportment are all the same from one person to the next. Social status, personal wealth, educational status, and personal or family connections no longer matter in that moment. People on fire all act the same. They all move the same. Anyone coming in contact with fire will have the same markings on their bodies, regardless of age or gender.

Intimacy with the Fire

Job chapter 42 and verse 5
"I have heard of Thee by the hearing of the ear (learned knowledge *of* God), *but now mine eye seeth Thee* (now I have intimate, first-hand, experiential knowledge of You)."
(KJV)

The fire of God's love, His Fire, not only consumes us, it also enlightens us. When we allow the fire of God to overtake and purify us, we will experience first-hand all that we have been taught and have believed by faith. We will be privileged to see and experience the very essence of God as never before.

Matthew chapter 5 and verse 8
Blessed are the pure in heart, for they will see God.
(NIV)

The more our flesh and the mortal humanity are stripped away from us, the clearer we will be able to see Him. Purity is a prerequisite for seeing Him. Only when our soul and spirit are cleansed, can God's light shine forth and we'll be able to see Him.

Hebrews chapter 12 and verse 14
Follow peace with all men, and holiness, without which no man shall see the Lord.

(KJV)

The presence of God is only seen through faith, not through our own abilities or our own understanding. By faith, we will see Him in every circumstance; by faith, we will be conscious of His closeness all the time; by faith, we will be trying to please Him in all we do; and by faith we will try to be moved only by His Spirit. Just like Moses, our goal should not simply be the security of our salvation, but the ability to see God face to face. Moses was so touched and so changed by the encounter that his face shown. His face shone on the outside because of what was happening to him on the inside. And the same thing can occur with us. Maybe, not to the degree that it happened with Moses, but we all have met those special people whose countenance glows because they have been with Jesus. They have been in the presence of God and it shows on the outside.

In this wonderful state of seeing and experiencing and knowing God's presence, we will begin to watch Him repay our painful times with His unfathomable love and affection. We will also begin to realize that in our dark seasons, He never really left us at all. He had to do what He did in order to get us to this point of intimacy. When we seek fellowship with the Fire, what we see with our natural eyes is swallowed up by faith, we see God in deeper more meaningful ways, our hope grows stronger, our faith grows more active, and our prayers are answered. Glory and amen!

Ephesians chapter 3 and verses 14-19
(14.) For this cause I bow my knees unto the Father of our Lord Jesus Christ,

(15.) Of whom the whole family in heaven and earth is named,

(16.) That He would grant you, according to the riches of His glory, to be strengthened with might by His Spirit in the inner man;

(17.) That Christ may dwell in your hearts by faith; that ye, being rooted and grounded in Love,

(18.) May be able to comprehend with all saints what is the breadth, and length, and depth, and height;

(19.) And, to know the Love of Christ, which passeth knowledge, that ye might be filled with all the fullness of God.

(KJV)

CHANGING A NATION;
SHAPING A GENERAION

With four words, three men changed forever a nation and firmly shaped a generation. The men were known as Shadrach, Meshach and Abednego, and their resounding words were, "I WILL NOT BOW."

Daniel chapter 3 and verse 1-30

(1.) Nebuchadnezzar the king [caused to be] made an image of gold, whose height was sixty cubits or ninety feet and its breadth six cubits or nine feet. He set it up on the plain of Dura in the province of Babylon.

(2.) Then Nebuchadnezzar the king sent to gather together the satraps, the deputies, the governors, the judges and chief stargazers, the treasurers, the counselors, the sheriffs and lawyers, and all the chief officials of the provinces to come to the dedication of the image which King Nebuchadnezzar had [caused to be] set up.

(3.) Then the satraps, the deputies, the governors, the judges and chief stargazers, the treasurers, the counselors, the sheriffs and lawyers, and all the chief officials of the provinces were gathered together for the dedication of the image that King Nebuchadnezzar had set up, and they stood before the image that Nebuchadnezzar had set up.

(4.) Then the herald cried aloud, You are commanded, O peoples, nations, and languages,

(5.) That when you hear the sound of the horn, pipe, lyre, trigon, harp, dulcimer or bagpipe, and every kind of music, you are to fall down and worship the golden image that King Nebuchadnezzar has set up.

(6.) And whoever does not fall down and worship shall that very hour be cast into the midst of a burning fiery furnace.

(7.) Therefore, when all the peoples heard the sound of the horn, pipe, lyre, trigon, dulcimer or bagpipe, and every kind of music, all the peoples, nations, and languages fell down and worshiped the golden image that King Nebuchadnezzar had set up.

(8.) Therefore at that time certain men of Chaldean descent came near and brought [malicious] accusations against the Jews.

(9.) They said to King Nebuchadnezzar, O king, live forever!

(10.) You, O king, have made a decree that every man who hears the sound of the horn, pipe, lyre, trigon, harp, dulcimer

or bagpipe, and every kind of music shall fall down and worship the golden image,

(11.) And that whoever does not fall down and worship shall be cast into the midst of a burning fiery furnace.

(12.) There are certain Jews whom you have appointed and set over the affairs of the province of Babylon—Shadrach, Meshach, and Abednego. These men, O king, pay no attention to you; they do not serve your gods or worship the golden image which you have set up.

(13.) Then Nebuchadnezzar in rage and fury commanded to bring Shadrach, Meshach, and Abednego; and these men were brought before the king.

(14.) [Then] Nebuchadnezzar said to them, Is it true, O Shadrach, Meshach, and Abednego, that you do not serve my gods or worship the golden image which I have set up?

(15.) Now if you are ready when you hear the sound of the horn, pipe, lyre, trigon, harp, dulcimer or bagpipe, and every kind of music to fall down and worship the image which I have made, very good. But if you do not worship, you shall be cast at once into the midst of a burning fiery furnace, and who is that god who can deliver you out of my hands?

(16.) Shadrach, Meshach, and Abednego answered the king, O Nebuchadnezzar, it is not necessary for us to answer you on this point.

(17.) If our God Whom we serve is able to deliver us from the burning fiery furnace, He will deliver us out of your hand, O king.

(18.) But if not, let it be known to you, O king, that we will not serve your gods or worship the golden image which you have set up!

(19.) Then Nebuchadnezzar was full of fury and his facial expression was changed [to antagonism] against Shadrach, Meshach, and Abednego. Therefore he commanded that the furnace should be heated seven times hotter than it was usually heated.

(20.) And he commanded the strongest men in his army to bind Shadrach, Meshach, and Abednego and to cast them into the burning fiery furnace.

(21.) Then these [three] men were bound in their cloaks, their tunics or undergarments, their turbans, and their other clothing, and they were cast into the midst of the burning fiery furnace.

(22.) Therefore because the king's commandment was urgent and the furnace exceedingly hot, the flame and sparks from the fire killed those men who handled Shadrach, Meshach, and Abednego.

(23.) And these three men, Shadrach, Meshach, and Abednego, fell down bound into the burning fiery furnace.

(24.) Then Nebuchadnezzar the king [saw and] was astounded, and he jumped up and said to his counselors, Did we not cast three men bound into the midst of the fire? They answered, True, O king.

(25.) He answered, Behold, I see four men loose, walking in the midst of the fire, and they are not hurt! And the form of the fourth is like a son of the gods!

(26.) Then Nebuchadnezzar came near to the mouth of the burning fiery furnace and said, Shadrach, Meshach, and Abednego, you servants of the Most High God, come out and come here. Then Shadrach, Meshach, and Abednego came out from the midst of the fire.

(27.) And the satraps, the deputies, the governors, and the king's counselors gathered around together and saw these men—that the fire had no power upon their bodies, nor was the hair of their head singed; neither were their garments scorched or changed in color or condition, nor had even the smell of smoke clung to them.

(28.) Then Nebuchadnezzar said, Blessed be the God of Shadrach, Meshach, and Abednego, Who has sent His angel and delivered His servants who believed in, trusted in, and relied on Him! And they set aside the king's command and yielded their bodies rather than serve or worship any god except their own God.

(29.) Therefore I make a decree that any people, nation, and language that speaks anything amiss against the God of Shadrach, Meshach, and Abednego shall be cut in pieces and their houses be made a dunghill, for there is no other God who can deliver in this way!

(30.) Then the king promoted Shadrach, Meshach, and Abednego in the province of Babylon.

(AMP)

It's amazing to think that, with a firm grasp on the Knowledge of God and His Ways, coupled with a holy fear of the only all-powerful, supreme God, three young men shook a nation to its core, effectively changing its most revered values and shaping forever a generation as they outlined a pattern of relational living with Father God. Over the next few minutes we will endeavor to plunge again, and a little further, into the lives of these men that we may discover how they were able stand in the face of tyranny and so boldly proclaim the way of the Lord.

In order to walk in the ways of the Lord, you must be able to see the ways of the Lord. You cannot go where you have no sight. You cannot mimic that which you have not first observed. Patterns are for protégés. God is light. In Him is the Light of the world, and through Him men have their life.

St. John chapter 1 and verse 1-10
(1.) *In the beginning was the Word, and the Word was with God, and the Word was God.*

(2.) *The same was in the beginning with God.*

(3.) *All things were made by Him; and without Him was not anything made that was made.*

(4.) *In Him was Life: and that Life was the Light of men.*

(5.) *And the Light shineth in Darkness; and Darkness comprehended it not.*

(6.) *There was a man sent from God, whose name was John.*

(7.) *The same came for a witness, to bear witness of the Light, that ALL MEN through Him might believe.*

(8.) *He was not that Light, but was sent to bear witness of that Light.*

(9.) *That was the true Light, which Lighteth every man that cometh into the world.*

(10.) He was in the world and the world was made by Him, and the world knew Him not.

(KJV)

God, as described by St. John, "the one whom Jesus loved", is light and in Him is no shadow or darkness. Therefore, the ways of God are well lit. The path of God is illuminated and clearly defined. The ways of the Lord are not hard to discover; neither are they hard to follow. Many people today are living in "blind Christianity" journeying throughout their days hoping to make right choices and decisions. Oftentimes, many Christians live with more unanswered questions, should haves, and might-have-beens than they were ever designed to carry. Christians often do their best to avoid any type of obstacle or challenge along the road down which God is leading them while identifying problems as the enemy, challenges as unwanted, and crises as the final nail in the coffin of their destiny.

When reading the accounts of triumph as depicted in the book of Daniel, specifically in chapter three, we often tend to think of those who conquered seemingly unconquerable circumstances as being of better blood than us. Somehow we place them at a higher level of strength or robustness (due to the times in which they lived or the family to which they were born) than we possess in today's time. However, as you are about to discover it was not the strength of body, the family to which they were born, or any other natural characteristic that caused them to triumph. Rather, their strength and ability was ascertained through their knowledge of God and their relation to His ability. Shadrach, Meshach and Abednego didn't "just have an inward feeling" and therefore didn't bow. They didn't "just have their conscious speak to them" and as a result found the power to stand amidst a sea of those bowed prostrate to an idol. If that were so, with all our modern-day churches that are filled with great men and women of God we would have an army standing up to the idols and evils of today. If a good conscious is all it takes to stand where others fall, then you and I would have never bowed to pressures in our lives. It takes more than a good conscious to stand in the face of adversity. It takes revelation knowledge of the Word of God, which always brings about a new level of faith. It takes close communion with the Father, which always brings about absolute trust in the whispered personal promises of God, and it takes a dogged determination to see all that God has assured you of come to pass.

You cannot *receive* what God has for you, until you *know* what God has for you. You cannot develop a real, intimate relationship with God on the basis of refraining from trouble. A relationship with God cannot be developed to avoid evil, but rather to experience the goodness and wonder of God Almighty. People only become bored because they have failed to spend adequate time in the presence of God. The presence of God is the only thing which will ever exist that neither man nor any other being can ever fully discover the depth of.

Knowledge is Power

Shadrach, Meshach and Abednego knew something we do not. They had insight or revelation knowledge concerning some things that we do not. Let's go there. Attitude is everything. Attitude is your approach to

something. Have you ever been told you need to change your attitude? Have you noticed that it is absolutely impossible to change your attitude, especially on demand? That's because no one can control his or her attitude. Your attitude is controlled by what you see. Your perspective governs your attitude. This is so crucial. You see, Shadrach, Meshach and Abednego did not have an attitude of fear. Their approach was not one of fear. They didn't say, "We will not bow" as they stood their shaking in their sandals and hoping they were making the right decision. No, they stood with boldness and proclaimed, "As for us, there can be no compromise." How did they do this? The answer is found in the word study of the Hebrew word for crisis. Shadrach, Meshach and Abednego saw something in their crisis that today's Christians do not see. My friend, the way you view a problem is about to change. The way you look your giants in the eye will be forever changed in the next few moments.

Your attitude in facing a crisis in life will always determine how you come out on the other end. You can either welcome the crisis as an opportunity to mature and become stronger, or you can resent the crisis as an unwelcome intruder and become bitter. How are you doing in the crisis you are facing? I find it interesting that the Chinese word for *crisis* combines two characters: one for danger and the other for opportunity. Is it not true that a crisis not only alerts us to imminent danger but also provides previously unexplored opportunities? The Hebrew word for *crisis* carries much the same idea. The term literally means "a birthing stool." It refers to a piece of furniture upon which a Jewish woman would position herself in Old Testament times to aid in the delivery of her baby. To be sure, the stool was a place of pain and trauma. A woman in labor might feel as if she were being swallowed up by contractions. But at the end, travail gives way to the marvelous moment of new birth and in that moment agony turns to fulfillment.

In the same way, a crisis in life can actually midwife a whole new set of blessings as our desperation pushes us into the arms of Jesus to discover His love and purpose for our lives. One of the most wonderful promises God gives His children is that absolutely nothing can touch our lives that He cannot work for our ultimate good

Romans chapter 8 and verse 28
And we know that in all things God works for the good of those who love him, who have been called according to his purpose.

(NIV)

Let's talk straight...I don't need to go into the details of childbirth. You have probably been there in one way or another. The glamour and glow of a pregnant woman is striking. From the moment of conception all is good until that last month... pressure everywhere. A pregnant woman can't sit right, and she will often walk with a little swagger. Did anyone really tell you or your wife the truth about childbirth? When a crisis enters our lives, we can panic. It's painful. We didn't plan for it to happen, and no one prepared us for change and pain. The Hebrew word for crisis is *messier.* Remember, this word describes a stool that Jewish women used to give birth to their children, a birthing stool. When we are in a crisis, we have to use this as a place for God to birth new things in our lives. We are now each a candidate for new possibilities and areas of the unknown that we would have never ventured into if we would have known the cost. Something good has to come out of it! Birthing pains produce new life. If we can endure, the joy will come in the morning. Also, the Word says that His mercies are new every morning. Be encouraged that this is just a test, and time will bring healing as new life springs forth out of your crisis. He has allowed you to be there "for such a time as this". When the heat is on, God shows up in the fire.

You see, Shadrach, Meshach and Abednego were not in wonder or question concerning the *Inferno Experience* that awaited them. They knew that this was the moment that they had been preparing for. Oftentimes we pray, *"Lord use me. Send me where you want me to go. Lord, have your prefect way in my life. Lord, whatever it takes, save my family. Lord, change this nation and shape this generation."* However, we are too often unprepared for the crisis, or as we have learned, opportunity God brings our way. God will answer your prayers no matter how extravagant they may seem. "Lord use me to change the world." But, know this: God will always bring the answer to your prayer in the form of a crisis.

He did so with Mary, the mother of Jesus. Mary was pledged to be married, but the angel of the Lord caused her to become pregnant by the supernatural seed of God. During the time of Mary and Joseph, if a lady was engaged to be married but did not remain faithful to her pledge, she would be put to death. Mary could have been stoned, but God made a way out of her tragedy. I encourage you to study the Bible. Every destiny was birthed from a tragedy:

-Moses through the abortionist.

-Abraham through many hostile armies, famine and bareness.

-Seth through the murder of his older brother.

-Noah through the great flood.

-Samuel through bareness.

-Elijah through Jezebel.

-David through Golioth.

-Jeremiah through the fall of Jerusalem.

-Eziekel through the conquest of Israel.

-The children of Israel through the Red Sea, many plagues, hostile nations, wars, famine, snakes and thirst.

The list goes on and on. Throughout the Bible as a whole, every great man and woman of God was birthed into their destiny through some kind of major tragedy. God is not trying to kill you. He's trying to open doors to your destiny. God is not only allowing your tragedy to happen to you, He has orchestrated it for the birthing of your new season. Allow God to perfect you through the storm. The next time you find yourself faced with a crisis, know you're right in the middle of a contraction, seated on the holy birthing stool of God, about to enter the greatest season of your life!

THE POWER TO BE CHANGED IS THE POWER TO BREAK CHAINS

When you think of chains, what do you think of? I'm not talking about the physical chains that are used to hold something in place. I'm talking about the spiritual chains that are holding you down. These could include cutting, pornography, addictions, drugs, alcohol, anorexia, and bulimia. These chains are anything that is holding you back, any secrets that you don't tell anyone about because you are so ashamed of them. But God knows them.

At one point in my life, I was bound by many of these chains with an unshakable feeling of being worthless, stuck in that dark pit of depression. These things were suffocating me like the chains were wrapped around my neck, and I was hanging there. I reached a breaking point where I couldn't move on. I was stuck there. I literally could only cry out to God and just ask him to break my chains.

"There is power in the name of Jesus, to break every chain." That is so true.

Colossians chapter 2 and verses 1-5
(1.) *For I want you to know how great a struggle I have for you and for those at Laodicea and for all who have not seen me face to face,*

(2.) *that their hearts may be encouraged, being knit together in love, to reach all the riches of full assurance of understanding and the knowledge of God's mystery, which is Christ,*

(3.) *in whom are hidden all the treasures of wisdom and knowledge.*

(4.) *I say this in order that no one may delude you with plausible arguments.*

(5.) *For though I am absent in body, yet I am with you in spirit, rejoicing to see your good order and the firmness of your faith in Christ.*

(ESV)

I needed to discover the great mystery of God, that is Christ. I in my own strength had no power over the spiritual chains by which I was trapped, but Christ has the power to break *all* chains. When I delved deeper in my commitment to him and endeavored to uncover the mysteries of Christ, He transformed me into a new creation, free from all that had me bound.

Romans chapter 8 and verses 1-17

(1.) *Therefore, there is now no condemnation for those who are in Christ Jesus,*

(2.) *because through Christ Jesus the law of the Spirit who gives life has set you free from the law of sin and death.*

(3.) *For what the law was powerless to do because it was weakened by the flesh, God did by sending his own Son in the likeness of sinful flesh to be a sin offering. And so he condemned sin in the flesh,*

(4.) *in order that the righteous requirement of the law might be fully met in us, who do not live according to the flesh but according to the Spirit.*

(5.) *Those who live according to the flesh have their minds set on what the flesh desires; but those who live in accordance with the Spirit have their minds set on what the Spirit desires.*

(6.) *The mind governed by the flesh is death, but the mind governed by the Spirit is life and peace.*

(7.) *The mind governed by the flesh is hostile to God; it does not submit to God's law, nor can it do so.*

(8.) *Those who are in the realm of the flesh cannot please God.*

(9.) You, however, are not in the realm of the flesh but are in the realm of the Spirit, if indeed the Spirit of God lives in you. And if anyone does not have the Spirit of Christ, they do not belong to Christ.

(10.) But if Christ is in you, then even though your body is subject to death because of sin, the Spirit gives life because of righteousness.

(11.) And if the Spirit of him who raised Jesus from the dead is living in you, he who raised Christ from the dead will also give life to your mortal bodies because of his Spirit who lives in you.

(12.) Therefore, brothers and sisters, we have an obligation— but it is not to the flesh, to live according to it.

(13.) For if you live according to the flesh, you will die; but if by the Spirit you put to death the misdeeds of the body, you will live.

(14.) For those who are led by the Spirit of God are the children of God.

(15.) The Spirit you received does not make you slaves, so that you live in fear again; rather, the Spirit you received brought about your adoption to sonship. And by him we cry, "Abba, Father."

(16.) The Spirit himself testifies with our spirit that we are God's children.

(17.) Now if we are children, then we are heirs—heirs of God and co-heirs with Christ, if indeed we share in his sufferings in order that we may also share in his glory.

(NIV)

Illustration

Arthur Conan Doyle, the ingenious creator of the Sherlock Holmes mysteries, once found great humor in a practical joke he played on 12 famous friends. Each of these men was virtuous and highly respected. For the joke, Doyle sent every one of them the same telegram: "Fly at once, all is discovered!" Within 24 hours, the dozen men of noble reputation had taken a trip out of the country! No matter how noble our reputation is, we all have things for which we are ashamed and hope no one discovers. The only lasting solution to a guilty conscience is the forgiveness of God Himself.

In the next few moments, we're going to deal with our failures. Sin is an obvious failure for us. What God would hope is not that we would dwell on our failures, but rather that we'd learn something from them. In fact, before we become buried in guilt, I'd like you to keep this story in mind as we tackle the tough topic of sin.

Illustration

A Louisiana farmer's favorite mule fell into a well. After studying the situation, the farmer came to the conclusion that he couldn't pull the mule out, so he might as well bury him. It would be the humane thing to do. So he got a truckload of dirt, backed up to the well, and dumped the dirt on top of the mule at the bottom of the well. But when the dirt hit the mule, it started snorting and tramping. As it tramped, it began to work itself up on top of the dirt. So the farmer continued to pour dirt in the well until the mule snorted and tramped its way to the top. It then walked away, a dirtier, but wiser mule. What was intended to bury it turned out to be its salvation.

Being stuck in a deep well of sin and its consequences is a terrible experience.

The Destructive Power of Sin

Part of the beauty of Romans 8 comes from its position in Paul's letter. In the preceding chapter, Paul takes a look at his own life, and his own shortcomings, and writes words like these:

Romans chapter 7 and verses 15, 18-19 & 24
(15.) I do not understand what I do. For what I want to do I do not do, but what I hate I do.

...

(18.) For I know that good itself does not dwell in me, that is, in my sinful nature. For I have the desire to do what is good, but I cannot carry it out.

(19.) For I do not do the good I want to do, but the evil I do not want to do—this I keep on doing.

...

(24.) What a wretched man I am! Who will rescue me from this body that is subject to death?

(NIV)

Had Paul ended his letter at that moment, it would have been one of the most depressing things any of us have ever read- not necessarily because we're disappointed in Paul, but because it rings so true in each of our hearts. We know we are a sinful people.

Illustration

Dr. Bob Reccord tells the story of a major move that was set to take place inside the halls of a Fortune 500 company. It was unheard of, but the company was ready to promote a 38-year-old from vice president to president. The young man was a very impressive businessman who wooed and awed the board of directors. Upon completing the final interview process, the board broke for lunch with plans to offer this man the prestigious position.

The young man went to lunch alone that day and was unintentionally followed by several of the board members, who happened to stand in line behind him. Naturally, they were watching him closely, filled with pride and excitement about the coming announcement. Just then, everything changed. When the young man came to the bread section, he placed two, 3-cent butter patties on his tray and nonchalantly covered them up with his napkin.

When he paid for his meal, he did not reveal the stolen treasures.

An hour later, a room that should have been filled with joy was instead marked by anger, and instead of being promoted to president, the young man with the promising future was fired - all for six cents worth of butter.

The smallest of our sins is costly, far more costly than any of us have ever imagined. Thankfully, Paul turned his attention away from his own sin, and back to the One who set him free from sin.

God Has Broken the Power of Sin

Paul says that God has already set him free from the law of sin and death (8:1), and that while he couldn't beat the sin that had hounded him, God did by sending his own Son. This is coming from a chapter-seven man who still battled sinful leanings, a man who often lost those battles. This should be a relief to us. God has already done the hard work in tackling the sin problem. Because of the cross, sin is defeated. Satan's greatest threat to any of us is a permanent separation from God because of our own sin. Satan sets the trap, and hopes we'll fall into it. But when Jesus gave his life up for the sake of sinners, the ultimate power of sin was defeated once and for all. Even though all of us have sinned and fallen short of God's glory (Romans 3:23), when we accept the gift of God's grace we can still experience God's glory as if we had never sinned at all.

Illustration

While staying with friends, I watched their hamster in his little cage. He has a warm nest of cedar shavings to curl up in, a water bottle to drink from, and best of all, a wheel he can run inside of. He has everything a hamster could want or need, but he refuses to run inside his running wheel. Instead, he has come up with what he thinks is a better idea. He climbs on top of the wheel, turns over on his back, and stretches out. Gradually the wheel starts to turn, and his entire body rolls with it, head first. The wheel picks up speed and spins faster and faster until CLUNK! His head smacks on the bottom of the cage. He gets up, shakes himself, apparently hurt from the unexpected sharp blow on his head.

But what does he do? He climbs back up on top of the wheel, turns over, stretches himself out, and gets ready to clunk his head again. Why? Why would a hamster that has everything he needs disregard the wheel's proper use and do something that only hurts himself? And why, even after that, would he do it again?

The bigger question is: Why do humans, who are supposedly smarter than hamsters, sometimes do the same thing?

Illustration

Tom Watson, Sr., is the man who founded IBM. You can imagine the money, the investments, the experiments, this man and his multi-billion dollar company have made through the years. Once, years ago, when a million dollars

131

was still a million dollars, Watson had a top junior executive who spent $12 million of the company's money on a venture that failed. The executive put his resignation on Watson's desk saying, *"I'm sure that you want my resignation."* Watson roared back, *"No I don't want your resignation. I've just spent $12 million educating you. It's about time you get to work."*

God won't accept your resignation. Instead, He'll accept your failures as part of the investment He has made in your spiritual growth. But now, He expects you to get to work. So let's do it.

Refuse the Power of Sin

According to what Paul writes in the book of Romans, the mind set on what our sinful nature desires will live by that sinful nature. On the other hand, if we set our minds on what the Spirit desires, we will live according to the Spirit. One mindset leads to death, and the other leads to life. One mindset leads to hostility with God, but the other leads to peace with God.

Romans chapter 8 and verses 5-8
(5.) Those who live according to the flesh have their minds set on what the flesh desires; but those who live in accordance with the Spirit have their minds set on what the Spirit desires.

(6.) The mind governed by the flesh is death, but the mind governed by the Spirit is life and peace.

(7.) The mind governed by the flesh is hostile to God; it does not submit to God's law, nor can it do so.

(8.) Those who are in the realm of the flesh cannot please God. (NIV)

The first psalm teaches the same principle, only with a different word picture.

Psalm 1 and verses 1-2
(1.) How happy is the man who does not follow the advice of the wicked or take the path of sinners or join a group of mockers!

(2.) Instead, his delight is in the LORD's instruction, and he meditates on it day and night.

(HCSB)

A man who meditates on the Word of God will delight himself and God, but a man who doesn't control his mind will slow first to a walk with the counsel of the wicked, then he will stand in the way of sinners, and finally, he will sit in the seat of mockers. We should run a good race for Christ, not even slowing to a walk!

James chapter 1 and verses 13-15
(13.) When tempted, no one should say, "God is tempting me." For God cannot be tempted by evil, nor does he tempt anyone;

(14.) but each person is tempted when they are dragged away by their own evil desire and enticed.

(15.) Then, after desire has conceived, it gives birth to sin; and sin, when it is full-grown, gives birth to death.

(NIV)

If you could go backwards through the progressive steps - from death to sin, from sin to the birth of sin, from the birth of sin to the desire to sin - you'll come to the point of your own evil desires. If at that point we take hold of the mind of Christ, we can break the progressive chain and stop its destructive cycle.

Paul says the key is to set our minds on what the Spirit desires. Is that a bad thing? The tempter would have us think that we've just missed out on some great experience, that God has actually punished us for leading a life of sin. But picture this: When a man and woman fall in love and get married, they automatically stop some practices and start others. For instance, both the husband and wife stop dating other people, and start enjoying the companionship for which they had so long searched.

Later in Romans, Paul writes these words to those who want to please God:

Romans chapter 12 and verse 2
Do not conform to the pattern of this world, but be transformed by the renewing of your mind. Then you will be able to test and approve what God's will is—his good, pleasing and perfect will.

(NIV)

Your transformed mind will make all the difference when it comes to enjoying or despising your walk with Christ. The power to break free from the chains of sin, the power that God has already provided, is already available to us, right now.

Illustration

Just before he was executed for his terrible crimes, mass murderer Ted Bundy told James Dobson that his road to prison had begun with a look at a pornographic magazine. Porn was immediately addictive for him, and it led to actions that were an affront to God and society. On the other hand, author and pastor Max Lucado took control of his mind and walked away from a potential problem with alcoholism. Lucado said, *"I come from a family of alcoholism. If there's anything about this DNA stuff, I've got it."* For more than 20 years, drinking wasn't a major issue for Lucado. But in 2001, it nearly became one. Lucado recalled, *"I lowered my guard a bit. One beer with a barbecue won't hurt. Then another time with Mexican food. Then a time or two with no food at all."*

One afternoon on his way to speak at a men's retreat he began to plot: *"Where could I buy a beer and not be seen by anyone I know?"* He drove to an out-of-the-way convenience store, parked, and waited till all the patrons left. He entered, bought a beer, held it close to his side, and hurried to his car. *"I felt a sense of conviction,"* Lucado remembers, *"because the night before I'd had a long talk with my oldest daughter about not covering things up."*

Lucado didn't drink that beer. Instead he rolled down the window, threw it in a trash bin, and asked God for forgiveness. He also decided to come clean with the elders of his church about what happened: *"When I shared it with the elders, they just looked at me across the table and said, 'Satan is determined to get you for this right now. We're going to cover this with prayer, but you've got to get the alcohol out of your life.' And I really took that as from God."*

Live Powerfully Apart from Sin

How you live is going to make a difference in the way you enjoy life.

Romans chapter 8 and verses 12-14
(12.) Therefore, brothers and sisters, we have an obligation— but it is not to the flesh, to live according to it.

(13.) For if you live according to the flesh, you will die; but if by the Spirit you put to death the misdeeds of the body, you will live.

(14.) For those who are led by the Spirit of God are the children of God.

(NIV)

Take the example of sexuality. A lifestyle of sexual sin can lead to embarrassment, physical and medical ramifications, financial penalties, and a guilt-ridden sense of spiritual bankruptcy. On the other hand, a lifestyle that honors God's plan for sexuality, and the rules He has placed around it, can enrich a marriage and create joy.

Controlling your mind and making progress in the battle against temptation become evident as we manifest spiritual fruit: love, joy, peace, patience, kindness, goodness, faithfulness, gentleness and self-control. Those rewards are worth the effort. Having a powerful way to live is worth the battle. With all this concentration on sin, most of us are left with a bit of worry. Does God really have enough grace for a sinner like me?

Illustration

Author and Pastor Lee Strobel tells this story.

Shortly after the Korean War, a Korean woman had an affair with an American soldier, and she got pregnant. He went back to the United States, and she never saw him again. She gave birth to a little girl who looked different than the other Korean children. She had light-colored, curly hair. In that culture, children of mixed race were ostracized by the community. In fact, many women would kill their children because they didn't want them to face such rejection. But this woman didn't do that. She tried to raise her little girl as best she could, until the rejection was too much. She did something that probably most could never imagine doing. She abandoned her little girl to the streets.

This little girl was ruthlessly taunted by people. They called her the ugliest word in the Korean language, "tooki", meaning *alien devil*. It didn't take long for this little girl to draw conclusions about herself based on the way people treated her. For two years she lived in the streets, until finally she made her way to an orphanage. One day, word came that a couple from America was going to adopt a little boy. All the children in the orphanage got excited, because at least one little boy was going to have hope. He was going to have a family. So this little girl spent the day cleaning up the little boys, giving them baths and combing their hair, and wondering which one would be adopted by the American couple.

The next day the couple came, and this is what the girl recalled:

"It was like Goliath had come back to life. I saw the man with his huge hands lift up each and every baby. I knew he loved every one of them as if they were his own. I saw tears running down his face, and I knew if they could, they would have taken the whole lot home with them. He saw me out of the corner of his eye. Now let me tell you, I was nine years old, but I didn't even weigh thirty pounds. I was a scrawny thing. I had worms in my body. I had lice in my hair. I had boils all over me. I was full of scars. I was not a pretty sight. But the man came over to me, and he began rattling away something in English, and I looked up at him. Then he took this huge hand and laid it on my face. What was he saying? He was saying, 'I want this child. This is the child for me.'"

With all our scars, with all that is wrong with us, with all the terrible consequences our sin has laid upon us, God still wants us. The cross is the proof. The only unknown is whether those who hear the invitation will accept the offer of adoption by God's love and grace.

"Love has the power to break all chains - Swim the deepest seas - Endure the strongest pains - Love is the glow in the darkest night leading you on until you have sight."

- Cristoto

"Being deeply loved by someone gives you strength, while loving someone deeply gives you courage."

- Lao Tzu
-

"Does love have responsibility and duty, and will it use those words? When you do something out of duty is there any love in it? In duty there is no love. The structure of duty in which the human being is caught is destroying him. So long as you are compelled to do something because it is your duty you don't love what you are doing. When there is love there is no duty and no responsibility."

- Jiddu Krishnamurti

"The beginning of love is to let those we love be perfectly themselves, and not to twist them to fit our own image. Otherwise we love only the reflection of ourselves we find in them."

- Thomas Merton

"Love is what we are born with. Fear is what we have learned here. The spiritual journey is the unlearning of fear and the acceptance of love back into our hearts."

- Marianne Williamson

2 Corinthians chapter 10 and verse 4
For the weapons of our warfare are not of the flesh but have divine power to destroy strongholds.

(ESV)

I don't know about the rest of you, but I have had some chains that need breaking. Actually I do know about the rest of you, because you are human, just like me. We all have weights and chains that hold us down, regardless of what they may be. The unbelieving world walks around completely unaware of the chains that subdue them. They think that they are free, when in reality they are in suffocating bondage to the evil spiritual forces of this world. But we, as believers in Christ, have had our minds illuminated by the Holy Spirit to see clearly the chains the enemy uses to bind us.

I have been through seasons throughout my years with the Lord where I felt as if I had shackles restraining my hands and feet. I've felt trapped in sin, unable to resist the sickening behaviors that I knew were inflicting damage on my soul. Whenever we get caught up in sin, many of us automatically think that we are not "eligible" to come to God and Him readily accept us. Naturally, we keep score of our *goodness* and *badness*. When we think that we are doing really well and keeping all the "rules", we feel as if we are acceptable to God and therefore step into His presence with boldness. But whenever we are not doing so well and give in to temptation and sin, we tend to tell ourselves that we need to wait a while and make ourselves better before we can come to God like we did before. This mentality is in complete opposition to the Gospel!

God accepts us, at ALL times, based on the merit and sacrifice of Jesus Christ. When you feel comfortable coming to God because of your "goodness", you're deceiving yourself into believing that your actions have made you desirable to God. In retrospect, because you have adopted this "works" mentality, you feel undesired by God whenever you're not doing so good. But let me remind you, your best works and behaviors are filthy rags to God. It was never, EVER, your goodness that made you acceptable to God. It was *Christ's* righteousness and *Christ's* bloodshed. It is *His* blood that makes you forgivable. It is *His* blood that makes you beautiful in the eyes of God. It is *His* blood that makes you acceptable to God and earns you entry into the presence of God. And *His* blood covers you at ALL times, not merely when your perception of your behavior has a gold star next to it. If you continue to remain outside the presence of God due to your feelings of inadequacy, you're going to continue to place yourself in the firing line of satan and his army of demons. They will relentlessly fire the bullets of false guilt and false shame at you. As long as they can keep you focusing on what you "do" and "don't do", the harder it will be for you to allow the real truth of the gospel to permeate your mind and restore your soul.

How does gospel truth restore your soul? By acknowledging this fact: your salvation has absolutely nothing to do with you (other than the fact that God loves you) and everything to do with Jesus Christ. God sent His Son into this world to live the life that you couldn't and wouldn't live, then appointed Him to suffer the death and wrath that you fully deserved to endure for your sins. This was not against the will of Jesus, but in perfect harmony with the sacrificial passion of Jesus, who willingly laid His life down for His sheep.

141

When you responded in faith to the finished work of Jesus, God cast all of your sins from His sight, along with your guilt and shame. Your eternal security was set in stone at that moment as you were sealed by the Holy Spirit for the Day of Redemption. Jesus has done it all for you. He fulfilled the law by living a life unstained by sin in full obedience to God. Jesus always loved God the Father as He ought to be loved. And He gives His righteousness to you as a gift. You don't earn a gift by good behavior. You receive a gift. And you received this gift of eternal salvation from Jesus by placing your faith in Him. *"For by grace you have been saved through faith. And this is not your own doing; it is the gift of God"* (Ephesians 2:8).

Whenever you fall into sin, you must remember that the sin has been paid for, whatever it is. God has extended His grace to you in such a way that nothing you could ever do could separate you from Him again. He will never reject you, and you will not lose your salvation. There may be some of you that disagree with me on that, but the Bible disagrees with you my friend. If you want to live your life in constant fear that God is going to revoke His promise to save you, it's your prerogative, but I urge you to reconsider and accept this glorious gospel truth. You didn't do anything to earn your salvation or God's love, and there is nothing you can do to lose it. When I say Jesus did everything, I mean He did everything. He purchased you with His blood and that blood will not fail you. There will always be forgiveness for those covered by the blood.

When you fail God, as we all do, refuse to listen to the lies of the enemy and run to your Savior. Run to Jesus!

Because He has forgiven you and loves you no less, no matter what you have done. Therein lies the power of breaking every chain. The fact that you are completely and eternally forgiven will always produce life in your spirit and hope in your heart, leading you to sincere repentance by which the power of the sin that once chained you down is eliminated.

This may seem too gracious of a Gospel to some of you. And I hope it does because the true Gospel of Jesus Christ is scandalously gracious.

But I will end with these two thoughts:

1) If you see this glorious grace of God as a license to continue on with your sin with no remorse, you have not been converted and are dead in your sins. Genuine faith will result in a life of good works and a pursuit of holiness.

2) In the words of Ben Pirtle, *"This message is for genuine believers in Jesus Christ, sons and daughters of God. If you are not covered by His sacrifice, you need to know that you are going to hell, and the shame and guilt you feel is very real."*

CHAPTER 10

POPULAR
OR POWERFUL

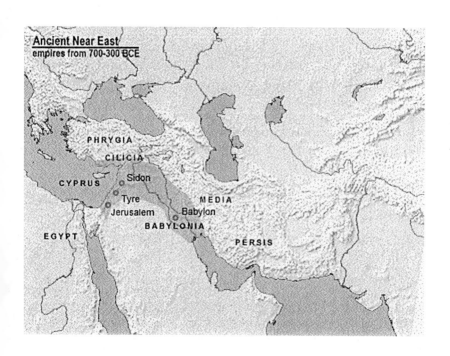

Ancient Near East
empires from 700-300 BCE

Daniel, like many of the young people in America today, was born in a time when his nation had turned its back on the Lord and were serving false gods and living godless lives. The Prophet Jeremiah was called by the Lord to warn the nation to repent and return to the Lord or face severe judgment at the hands of the Babylonian armies, and for forty years he was faithful to his heavenly calling. His repeated warnings to his nation fell on deaf ears and hard hearts, but in the midst of it all scripture tells us of at least six different people whom Jeremiah, a contemporary of Daniel, must have influenced (Baruch, Jeremiah's personal secretary, the Prophet Habakkuk, Daniel and his three Hebrew fellow captives) which kept the torch of faith lit for the coming generations. It is more than likely that Jeremiah may not have even realized that his ministry had influenced this handful of people, four of which were just teenagers, who would rise to become great heroes of the faith.

One of these six was the Prophet Habakkuk, who the Lord called to publish a written warning to the nation about twenty years after Jeremiah began his preaching ministry.

Habakkuk chapter 2 and verse 2-3
(2.) Then the Lord replied: "Write down the revelation   and make it plain on tablets   so that a herald may run with it.

(3.) For the revelation awaits an appointed time;   it speaks of the end   and will not prove false.   Though it linger, wait for it;   it will certainly come   and will not delay.

(NIV)

About two years later and approximately 22 years into Jeremiah's ministry, King Nebuchadnezzar and his Babylonian army made their first of three raids on the nation of Judah. During this first raid Nebuchadnezzar captured several of the choice people and youth of the nation and took them as captives back to Babylon. Many of these would become menial slaves in the kingdom, but some of the choicest of the young men were put through three years of higher Babylonian education in which the students would have any and all of their past religious faith and loyalties erased from their hearts and minds and replaced with the faith of the false gods of the land, as well as learning the necessary subjects needed to be an administrator in the Kingdom. With this new faith also came the demand for a new and complete loyalty to the king and his government as supreme. Once their training was completed they would then be ready to take their place as equipped and trusted servants in Nebuchadnezzar's Kingdom.

Four of these youths were Daniel and the three Hebrew boys. Daniel and his companions were probably around the age of fifteen or sixteen years old when taken captive, making them born about six or seven years after Jeremiah

began his ministry to Judah. Of these four, Daniel becomes the most prominent, and the greatest example of how we as Christians are to live for Jesus as strangers in a foreign land.

America today, like Judah of Daniel's day, has forsaken the Lord and is now facing a similar fate as that of Judah. Like Daniel, this generation is faced with a different America than previous men and women. American culture today is in many ways similar to Babylonian culture. The powers that be are trying to cleanse the Lord from the minds and hearts of a generation and bring them into the cycle of a godless, God-forgotten society. Maybe no greater model exists today for this generation who seek to be true to Jesus in a godless world than Daniel. Let's recap Daniel's life in order to piece the contents of this book together and discover how to change a nation and shape a generation.

The very first things we see as we look at the life of Daniel are the challenges that he faced as a youth, one that was a believer desiring to live for the Lord. Every youth or developing follower of Christ faces many challenges. We must navigate those challenges with God responses, instead of rational reactions, like Daniel to leave a lasting impact. Daniel faced four particular challenges in his day. Lets take a peek at those challenges in hopes that we may learn from His responses and effectively duplicate his results.

The Challenge of a Secular Education

Daniel chapter 1 and verses 3-4
(3.) Then the king ordered Ashpenaz, chief of his court officials, to bring into the king's service some of the Israelites from the royal family and the nobility—

(4.) young men without any physical defect, handsome, showing aptitude for every kind of learning, well informed, quick to understand, and qualified to serve in the king's palace. He was to teach them the language and literature of the Babylonians.

(NIV)

Nebuchadnezzar knew that the first thing that had to be done was to win the minds of a still forming generation. To do this they would be placed in a secular education system in which their God, the True and Living God was eliminated, and humanism and secularism would be drummed into their minds until they had been transformed from a Christian worldview to a secular worldview.

Notice that this is what the spirit of this age through the form and function of those who label themselves secular humanists has sought to do in this generation. Since the 1960s, the Bible and prayer have been eliminated from our educational system and have been replaced with the doctrines of humanism and secularism.

Abraham Lincoln said that the philosophy of the generation in our schools today will be the philosophy of the generation that is running our government tomorrow, and that is where we are today in America. The generations that have been raised in our schools where the Bible and prayer have been removed are now the very people that are removing the Bible and prayer from the rest of our society.

The Challenge of Sinful Enticements

Daniel chapter 1 and verses 5 & 8
(5.) The king assigned them a daily amount of food and wine from the king's table. They were to be trained for three years, and after that they were to enter the king's service.

...

(8.) But Daniel resolved not to defile himself with the royal food and wine, and he asked the chief official for permission not to defile himself this way.

(NIV)

Nebuchadnezzar, like satan, had enough smarts to understand that it would be much easier to win the still forming generation over to his gods and government if he baited the hook with attractive, sinful enticements. The king's wine and meat, not the common food of these young men, but the kings own rations, were offered them. Yet, Daniel's God had said in His Word that these things were sinful for the people of God to partake of. The generation of our day is being lured to satan's side by more sinful enticements than any other generation has ever known. Sex, drugs, alcohol, pornography, and on and on we can go.

This generation cannot turn the television on without being bombarded with sex, alcohol, and every form of sin imaginable. Anyone can get on the Internet and for free, pull up and watch the most vile, degrading sex acts imaginable. The eyes of this generation are steered to model their role models: teachers, politicians, entertainers, sports figures, and even parents living sinful and godless lives before them day in and day out.

The abundance of temptations, the poor role models, combined with a secular educational system, weak pulpits, and parents who are not the spiritual leaders to their children that they are meant to be are producing one lost generation after another until eventually our Christian heritage will be completely erased from our society. We are already seeing that very few leaders in our government today hold a Christian worldview. Not only do they not have a Christian worldview themselves, they are antagonistic towards all who do hold such views. It would seem as though Babylon is winning the battle for the minds and hearts of our children. The situation is so desperate that only a Holy Ghost, heaven-sent revival will save America. The light shines brightest in the darkest of moments. The vile and bold offensiveness of an enemy always signals a fresh mantel, new anointing that is descending from the hand of God upon a delivering generation.

The Challenge of Social Edicts

Daniel chapter 6 and verses 4-9
(4.) At this, the administrators and the satraps tried to find

grounds for charges against Daniel in his conduct of government affairs, but they were unable to do so. They could find no corruption in him, because he was trustworthy and neither corrupt nor negligent.

(5.) Finally these men said, "We will never find any basis for charges against this man Daniel unless it has something to do with the law of his God.

(6.) So these administrators and satraps went as a group to the king and said: "May King Darius live forever!

(7.) The royal administrators, prefects, satraps, advisers and governors have all agreed that the king should issue an edict and enforce the decree that anyone who prays to any god or human being during the next thirty days, except to you, Your Majesty, shall be thrown into the lions' den.

(8.) Now, Your Majesty, issue the decree and put it in writing so that it cannot be altered—in accordance with the law of the Medes and Persians, which cannot be repealed."

(9.) So King Darius put the decree in writing.

(NIV)

Daniel was forced to live in a society that had now outlawed his faith. It was now against the law of the land to pray to his God and to publicly practice his faith. What a similar world we live in, where prayer and the Bible are all but totally banned from our society by law along with the symbols of our faith, such as the Cross, nativity displays, and the Ten Commandments, but we are not talking about the former Soviet Union or the godless Russia of today. This is reality in America, the nation that once boasted of her exceptionalism and Christian heritage. This generation, like Daniel, is facing the challenges of secular education, sinful enticements, and social edicts that now all but make Christianity an outlawed faith in the land of so-called religious freedom.

The Challenge of the Suffering Entailed

Daniel chapter 6 and verses 10-23

(10.) Now when Daniel learned that the decree had been published, he went home to his upstairs room where the windows opened toward Jerusalem. Three times a day he got down on his knees and prayed, giving thanks to his God, just as he had done before.

(11.) Then these men went as a group and found Daniel praying and asking God for help.

(12.) So they went to the king and spoke to him about his royal decree: "Did you not publish a decree that during the next thirty days anyone who prays to any god or human being except to you, Your Majesty, would be thrown into the lions' den?"

The king answered, "The decree stands—in accordance with the law of the Medes and Persians, which cannot be repealed."

(13.) Then they said to the king, "Daniel, who is one of the

exiles from Judah, pays no attention to you, Your Majesty, or to the decree you put in writing. He still prays three times a day."

(14.) When the king heard this, he was greatly distressed; he was determined to rescue Daniel and made every effort until sundown to save him.

(15.) Then the men went as a group to King Darius and said to him, "Remember, Your Majesty, that according to the law of the Medes and Persians no decree or edict that the king issues can be changed."

(16.) So the king gave the order, and they brought Daniel and threw him into the lions' den. The king said to Daniel, "May your God, whom you serve continually, rescue you!"

(17.) A stone was brought and placed over the mouth of the den, and the king sealed it with his own signet ring and with the rings of his nobles, so that Daniel's situation might not be changed.

(18.) Then the king returned to his palace and spent the night without eating and without any entertainment being brought to him. And he could not sleep.

(19.) At the first light of dawn, the king got up and hurried to the lions' den.

(20.) When he came near the den, he called to Daniel in an anguished voice, "Daniel, servant of the living God, has your God, whom you serve continually, been able to rescue you

from the lions?"

(21.) Daniel answered, "May the king live forever!

(22.) My God sent his angel, and he shut the mouths of the lions. They have not hurt me, because I was found innocent in his sight. Nor have I ever done any wrong before you, Your Majesty."

(23.) The king was overjoyed and gave orders to lift Daniel out of the den. And when Daniel was lifted from the den, no wound was found on him, because he had trusted in his God.
(NIV)

Entailed is a good word to describe the other challenge Daniel faced. Webster defines *entailed* as, "to require as a necessary consequence." The government had not only outlawed Daniel's faith. The law required that anyone found breaking it would be required to face the necessary consequences. For Daniel it would mean being thrown into a lion's den and being lied about and conspired against. For the three Hebrew boys, it would mean being thrown into the fiery furnace in an attempt to take their lives.

This generation of God followers is the first in American history asked to endure the threats posed by governmental power for practicing their faith. Many have been, in today's America, fined, imprisoned, slandered, fired and worse. Daniel, when told he could not pray by order of the law, went as had been his custom to his regular place and time of prayer and threw open his windows that all could see that he was continuing to practice his faith regardless of man's law or the consequences for breaking them. How many would dare to be Daniel when facing a similar or even lesser challenge?

The challenges Daniel faced as a devoted son of God, all alone in a foreign land are the same challenges facing this generation. In one way or another the spirit of this age is roaring, daring any to oppose its secular worldviews. That roar is soon to be answered by those of this generation that have answered the call to stand out from the status quo, and in doing so dare to shape a nation and change a generation.

Daniel chapter 1 and verse 8
But Daniel resolved not to defile himself with the royal food and wine, and he asked the chief official for permission not to defile himself this way.

(NIV)

Daniel's response to these challenges reveals that he was a man with some rock-ribbed convictions that he was not willing to compromise, no matter what the eventual cost may be. Therein lies the key to his ability to leave the mark that he was able to leave on his generation. Shallow convictions if properly evaluated will cause many to question whether they are really Christians. Let's look at some of Daniel's heart-felt, Christian convictions that we might adopt them and in so doing receive the power to forever change this generation and shape our nation in the image of God's Kingdom all for His glory.

Daniel's Convictions

1 John chapter 3 and verse 4
Everyone who sins breaks the law; in fact, sin is lawlessness.

(NIV)

Daniel knew what sin was and would not partake of the Kings wine and meat because the Word of God says that he was not to do so as a son of God. Daniel believed in the inspiration and authority of the Word of God. When it speaks, the Lord is speaking, and when it says that there were things we are to do and not to do, Daniel believed it would be sin to defy or ignore that commandment.

The majority of Americans today believe truth is relative. A thing that is wrong for you may not be for me, or a thing that is right for you may not be for me. We so often see this type of demonic thinking used as the rationale of the homosexual movement. There is nothing wrong with it if it is right for me, so live and let live. But God is raising up a generation of God-fearing men and women that have NO COMPROMISE in their spirit, people who will ascend the mountain of the Lord in worship in order to descend with the power to change this world for Jesus Christ.

Daniel believed in absolutes and in the authority of God's Word. If it said a thing was sin then to him it was sin, no matter what man or the laws of man said. This is the key to his unwavering, passionate following of his Maker. Many a people have tried to legalize what God has outlawed from the beginning. If God's Word calls it sin, it will always be sin, no matter what man may call it. That was a clear conviction of Daniel's. All who are reading this, *I Dare You To Be Daniel!*

++++++

Psalm 51 and verse 4
Against you, you only, have I sinned and done what is evil in your sight...

(NIV)

Daniel knew whom sin was against. He knew, as did King David, that sin was what God said it was and when he failed to do as God had said, it was not only a sin, but it was a sin against God Himself. That places sin in a different light if it be against the Lord Himself.

++++++
Daniel knew sin would eventually have dire consequences for the sinner.

Numbers chapter 32 and verse 23
But if you fail to do this, you will be sinning against the Lord; and you may be sure that your sin will find you out.

(NIV)

Galatians chapter 6 and verse 7
Be not deceived, God is not mocked, for whatever a man soweth, that shall he also reap.

(KJV)

Moses knew that the pleasures of sin were just for a season. *"He chose to be mistreated along with the people of God rather than to enjoy the fleeting pleasures of sin"* (Hebrews 11:25). That is why he turned his back on the world and refused to be called the son of Pharaoh's daughter. That life of sin was bound to end in destruction, and Moses got out before it destroyed him as it had already done to millions. Sinner, do not think for a moment that there will not be severe consequences for you if you break the commandments of the Lord. It is sin, and a Holy God cannot and will not tolerate any man willfully defying Him and His commandments. All sin leads eventually to dire consequences. This is the unwavering conviction that Daniel had about sin.

++++++

Daniel knew that the only atonement from sin's penalty and deliverance from sin's power was the blood of Jesus.

Romans chapter 1 and verse 16
(16.) For I am not ashamed of the gospel, because it is the power of God that brings salvation to everyone who believes: first to the Jew, then to the Gentile.

(NIV)

Hebrews chapter 9 and verse 22
(22.) In fact, the law requires that nearly everything be cleansed with blood, and without the shedding of blood there is no forgiveness.

(NIV)

1 John chapter 1 and verses 8-9
(8.) If we claim to be without sin, we deceive ourselves and the truth is not in us.

(9.) If we confess our sins, he is faithful and just and will forgive us our sins and purify us from all unrighteousness.
(NIV)

At least three times in Daniel's writing, he reveals how the coming anti-christ will *"...take away the daily sacrifice..."* in Jerusalem when he rules during the Tribulation period. This shows us that Daniel had a clear understanding that these sacrifices were a type and shadow of the coming Savior and the shedding of His blood during His death upon Calvary's cross for the sins of man. Daniel knew the only answer for man's sin was the blood of our Lord, Jesus Christ that would later be shed on Calvary's cross.

++++++

Daniel chapter 2 and verses 44-45
(44.) In the time of those kings, the God of heaven will set up a kingdom that will never be destroyed, nor will it be left to another people. It will crush all those kingdoms and bring them to an end, but it will itself endure forever.

(45.) This is the meaning of the vision of the rock cut out of a mountain, but not by human hands—a rock that broke the iron, the bronze, the clay, the silver and the gold to pieces.

The great God has shown the king what will take place in the future. The dream is true and its interpretation is trustworthy.

(NIV)

Daniel had convictions about the Lord's second coming. The Lord showed Daniel the course of history that will lead to the end, including the coming of the Lord to set up His Kingdom upon the earth after He has broken the powers of all the kingdoms of man. From the moment the Lord showed Daniel these facts, he embraced this blessed hope, and it had a tremendous impact on his entire life. It should impact our lives as well.

1 John chapter 3 and verse 3
All who have this hope in him purify themselves, just as he is pure.

(NIV)

The blessed hope will motivate us to live a pure life. Daniel knew that outside of Calvary nothing motivated a man to live a pure life as much as did the truth of the imminent return of Jesus for His own. If you knew you were going to have an important guest coming to your home soon, you would get your house in order and make sure it was spotless. That is the effect the blessed hope has upon true believers.

Philippians chapter 4 and verses 4-5
(4.) Rejoice in the Lord always. I will say it again: Rejoice!

(5.) Let your gentleness be evident to all. The Lord is near.

The blessed hope will keep your life from being filled with worry and anxieties. The coming again of the Lord Jesus tells us that the Lord is in complete control of the world as a whole and our individual worlds as well. We need not worry. We just need to be faithful to Jesus and claim His promises. The world may look out of control, but be at rest. Jesus is still on His throne. Daniel believed this with all of his heart, and we can rest in that assurance as well.

1 Thessalonians chapter 4 and verses 13-18
(13.) Brothers and sisters, we do not want you to be uninformed about those who sleep in death, so that you do not grieve like the rest of mankind, who have no hope.

(14.) For we believe that Jesus died and rose again, and so we believe that God will bring with Jesus those who have fallen asleep in him.

(15.) According to the Lord's word, we tell you that we who are still alive, who are left until the coming of the Lord, will certainly not precede those who have fallen asleep.

(16.) For the Lord himself will come down from heaven, with a loud command, with the voice of the archangel and with the trumpet call of God, and the dead in Christ will rise first.

(17.) After that, we who are still alive and are left will be caught up together with them in the clouds to meet the Lord in the air. And so we will be with the Lord forever.

(18.) Therefore encourage one another with these words.

(NIV)

    The blessed hope will comfort your heart when you stand at the gravesite of a loved one. The hope they are in Heaven with Jesus, *"...which is far better"* (Philippians 1:23) than being here upon this troubled earth gives comfort to every broken heart who will believe it. It is the sure hope that one day soon you will be together again. It's no wonder the Bible calls it *our blessed hope.*

Hebrews chapter 10 and verses 35-37
(35.) So do not throw away your confidence; it will be richly rewarded.

(36.) You need to persevere so that when you have done the will of God, you will receive what he has promised.

(37.) For, "In just a little while,   he who is coming will come and will not delay."

(NIV)

    The blessed hope will give you the motivation to faithfully endure the difficulties of this life, knowing that the Lord could come and put an end to our trials and suffering at any moment. Knowing that the Lord is at hand tells the believer that the best is yet ahead of us no matter the troubles we may be experiencing in the present. They will all come to an end at the return of Jesus, and that could be at any moment. A man can endure almost anything if he believes it will eventually come to an end. That is why Daniel was able to faithfully endure years of captivity and the many trials that came with it. No wonder Titus calls the coming of the Lord the blessed hope for the Christian.

++++++

Daniel had convictions about eternity:

Daniel chapter 12 and verses 1-3
(1.) At that time Michael, the great prince who protects your people, will arise. There will be a time of distress such as has not happened from the beginning of nations until then. But at that time your people—everyone whose name is found written in the book—will be delivered.

(2.) Multitudes who sleep in the dust of the earth will awake: some to everlasting life, others to shame and everlasting contempt.

(3.) Those who are wise will shine like the brightness of the heavens, and those who lead many to righteousness, like the stars forever and ever.

(NIV)

  Daniel saw that the souls of all men are eternal. Satan would like for you to believe that death will end it all, but the Bible is clear that, *"It is appointed unto man once to die, but after this the judgment"* (Hebrews 9:27). There is life after death and it begins with judgment. As we've discussed already, every man is created in the image of God. We are eternal beings, as is God. There was a time that you *were* not, but since your conception there will never again be a time when you *are* not!

Daniel saw that there was an eternal heaven awaiting the saved:

1 John chapter 2 and verse 17
And the world passeth away, and the lust of it; but he that doeth the will of God abideth forever.

(KJV)

This world we know is already doomed for judgment, and man is heading for death. So, the Lord has prepared another home for each eternal soul, for the redeemed, those who have put their trust in Jesus for salvation.

Jesus tells us in John 14:2-3, *"...I go to prepare a place for you. And if I go and prepare a place for you, I will come again, and receive you unto myself, that where I am, there ye may be also."* The Apostle Paul tells us in 2 Corinthians 5:6, *"...to be absent from the body, and to be present with the Lord."* Heaven is the eternal home for the sons and daughters of God. Daniel believed in a literal heaven where the saved go upon their death to be with Jesus and remain throughout eternity.

Daniel also believed the Lord had an eternal place for the soul of the unbeliever. That place is hell, and it is just as real as is heaven. Men go there just as they do heaven. I realize that many do not believe this fact any longer, but it is still in the BOOK, and people are still going there every day even though the Church and an already Christ-denying world refuse to believe in hell any longer.

++++++

Daniel chapter 12 and verses 2-3

(2.) Multitudes who sleep in the dust of the earth will awake: some to everlasting life, others to shame and everlasting contempt.

(3.) Those who are wise will shine like the brightness of the heavens, and those who lead many to righteousness, like the stars forever and ever.

(NIV)

Daniel had strong beliefs about salvation. It is evident throughout the Book of Daniel that Daniel did not believe like so many others, that a man lived and died and that was all there was, nor did he believe that all men end up in heaven eventually.

Romans chapter 3 and verse 23

... for all have sinned and fall short of the glory of God.

(NIV)

Acts chapter 4 and verse 12

Salvation is found in no one else, for there is no other name under heaven given to mankind by which we must be saved.

(NIV)

Daniel believed that ALL men MUST have their own personal salvation experience with Jesus, the Messiah. He did not believe that heaven was the automatic destiny for everyone. He believed ALL MEN MUST BE SAVED to escape hell and go to heaven. Daniel also believed, however, that no one will be excluded from being saved except those who refuse to come to Jesus and Him alone

166

for salvation. The books of St. John and 2 Peter confirm that salvation is both inclusive and exclusive:

St. John chapter 3 and verse 16
For God so loved the world, that he gave his only begotten Son, that whosoever believeth in him should not perish, but have everlasting life.

(KJV)

2 Peter chapter 3 and verse 9
The Lord is not slack concerning his promise, as some men count slackness; but is longsuffering to us-ward, not willing that any should perish, but that all should come to repentance.

(KJV)

"For God so loved the world, that He gave His only begotten Son, that WHOSOEVER (all inclusive) **BELIEVETH IN HIM** (exclusive to believers in Jesus only) should not perish, (go to hell), but have everlasting life." There is everlasting life in heaven for the believer, and everlasting damnation in hell for the unbeliever. That is what the Bible teaches, and that is the conviction that Daniel strongly held to.

St. John chapter 14 and verse 6
Jesus saith unto him, I am the way, the truth, and the life: no man cometh unto the Father, but by me.

(KJV)

Acts chapter 4 and verse 12
Neither is there salvation in any other: for there is none other name under heaven given among men, whereby we must be saved.

(KJV)

Romans chapter 10 and verse 13
For whosoever shall call upon the name of the Lord shall be saved.

(KJV)

Philippians chapter 2 and verses 9-11
(9.) Wherefore God hath also highly exalted him, and given him a name that is above every name:

(10.) That at the name of Jesus, every knee should bow, of things in heaven, and of things in earth, and things under the earth;

(11.) And that every tongue should confess that Jesus Christ is Lord, to the glory of God the Father.

(KJV)

Daniel believed all must be saved the same way. He believed strongly that there was salvation in none other than Jehovah God. There were no other gods in Daniel's belief system except the imaginary gods that evil men had created from their own evil imaginations. Daniel knew that salvation was only through faith in the coming Messiah, the Lamb of God, who would sacrifice His sinless life and shed His innocent blood on the Cross to atone for the sins of mankind. Daniel believed that salvation was exclusively in Christ alone. The Name of Jesus is the *ONLY NAME WHEREBY MEN MUST BE SAVED*. The Bible makes it crystal clear that the *only name* that a lost sinner can call upon for salvation is the *Name of Jesus*.

DANIEL'S COURAGE

Daniel chapter 6 and verse 10
Now when Daniel knew that the writing was signed, he went into his house; and his windows being open in his chamber toward Jerusalem, he kneeled upon his knees three times a day, and prayed, and gave thanks before his God, as he did aforetime.

(KJV)

Let's take a quick look at Daniel's courage. Daniel's convictions would have been of little value to him and to others if he had not possessed the *courage* of his convictions. That is one thing that is sorely missing among the Lord's people today. This lack of supernatural courage and boldness within the Church is one of the leading reasons that we are being defeated in every moral and spiritual battle we face in America today. Courage is a must if we are each going to be a faithful, obedient and victorious Christian in this day of increasing hostility towards Jesus and His Church.

Throughout history, a decline in the courage of any group marked the beginning of its end. That is why Jesus commanded His disciples in Acts chapter one not to depart from the upper room until they knew for certain that they had been filled and empowered by the Holy Spirit. The

169

powers of darkness waging war against the Church can only be met and overcome with the *power* and the *courage* of the convictions that only the fullness of the Holy Spirit can provide.

There was a day in America when temptations and opposition were far fewer than we face today. It did not take as much power for a Christian to live successfully for Jesus. Those days are gone, and today we find ourselves in circumstances similar to Daniel's day, and there is no way to maintain your victory over temptation and opposition without the power of God at work in your life. The Lord will only share His power with those to whom *HE IS REALLY LORD*. The ones to whom Jesus is ALL are the only ones who will know His power and victory in the days to come. Jesus will only fill the fully-submitted heart, never the half-hearted.

I once read about a young man who was crippled and confined to a wheelchair. In church one Sunday morning, he heard his pastor preach a challenging sermon on being sold out to Jesus. During the invitation time he wheeled himself to the altar. After arriving at the altar the young man asked the Pastor, *"Pastor, can the Lord use half a man?"* To this his Pastor replied, *"Son, the Lord can and will use half a man who is fully surrendered to Him, but He cannot and will not use a whole man who is half surrendered to Him."* That is why the lukewarm Church is so impotent today.

DANIEL'S COMPENSATION

Let me close by saying a word about Daniel's compensation. Daniel paid a price at times for his faithfulness to the Lord, but the Lord's compensation for his faithfulness far outweighed any price that he paid for remaining true to Jesus.

(A.) He enjoyed a *"Special Fellowship"* with Jesus that those who compromised never knew.

(B.) He enjoyed a *Special Favor* that Jesus continually gave him with others, especially those that were in positions of great power. None of the compromisers knew any of this favor in their lives.

(C.) He enjoyed a *Special Force* within his life. What I mean by this is Daniel's life was a force for the Lord; his short time here upon the earth was not a wasted life, but a force for Jesus. It could be said of Daniel what the Lord said of King David in Acts 13:36, *"...David...served his own generation by the will of God..."*

Nothing could be greater than to have the Lord use your life to be a force for Him while you are among the living. Too many Christians live and die and leave a hole, a void, behind them when they are gone. When you stick your hand in a bucket of water and pull it out, it doesn't take even a second for the hole to fill back up. That is the way it is for many Christians when they die. It doesn't take long for their absence to be filled by another. Their lives made little impact for Jesus and their absence is barely missed. The cost will no doubt get greater to live faithfully for Jesus in the days ahead, but my friend, as the life of Daniel shows, the compensation from the Lord will far outweigh the costs, not only in this life, but in the life to come.

Daniel chapter 12 and verses 2-3
(2.) Multitudes who sleep in the dust of the earth will awake: some to everlasting life, others to shame and everlasting contempt.

(3.) Those who are wise will shine like the brightness of the heavens, and those who lead many to righteousness, like the stars forever and ever.

(NIV)

CONCLUSION

In these days of increasing challenges to our Faith, we need Daniels who will not allow the world to mold them into its image, Daniels who are willing to hold to their convictions regardless of the challenges they may face or the consequences for doing so, Daniel's who have the courage of their convictions. We need Christians that are, *"...strong in the Lord, and in the power of His might"* (Ephesians 6:10); Christians who have, *"Put on the whole armor of God, that ye may be able to stand against the wiles of the devil"* (Ephesians 6:11); Christians who want to keep the torch of faith lit to pass on to their children and grandchildren; Christians who can say with the Apostle Paul: *"For our light affliction, which is but for a moment, working for us a far more exceeding and eternal weight of glory"* (2 Corinthians 4:17); Christians who want to come to the end of life and be able to say about their lives what the Apostle Paul said about his time here when he knew his time of departure was at hand: *"I have fought a good fight, I have finished my course, I have kept the faith; henceforth there is laid up for me a crown of righteousness, which the Lord, the righteous judge, shall give me at that day; and not to me only, but unto all them also that love His appearing"* (2 Timothy 4:7, 8).

INVITATION

I want to encourage each of you to examine your life and your loyalty to Jesus. Are you a Daniel, or are you like the thousands of other young men and women that were taken to Babylon along with Daniel and the three Hebrew boys. We never read about all of the other captives, and no doubt the reason we don't is because they were not willing to be Daniels. They were not willing to have the courage of their convictions and risk suffering for their faith. They preferred to compromise their faith rather than to suffer *for* their faith. If this is you, I beg you for your sake, for the sake of our nation, for the sake of your family, and for the Lord's sake to repent and rededicate your life to Jesus, surrender your all to Him, and allow Him to use you in this generation according to His will.

If you are lost, I want to encourage you to recognize that you are a sinner (Romans 3:23) and that the wages of sin is death (Romans 6:23). If you are not saved before you die or before the return of Jesus for His Church, you will eventually die and go to hell for all of eternity. But, no one has to die and go to hell. Christ Jesus died for you to pay for your sin (John 3:15; Romans 5:8). He rose from the grave and is no doubt speaking to your heart through this very book. If while you hear His voice, you reach out to Him with a repentant heart and call upon Him, He will save you this very moment (Romans 10:13). Then, you too may take up your cross and follow Jesus as Daniel did. You too can have a life that really matters. You too can live for more than success. You can live a life of significance, a life that will matter for a time and for eternity.

Author Biography

Jordan Bradford is a musician, charismatic leader, visionary, progressive thinker and entrepreneur with an incredible God-given ability to communicate the Gospel in fresh and creative ways. He is a dynamic leader, pressing the boundaries of "church as usual" to advance the Kingdom of God like never before.

Jordan's story is one of unusual significance. In a small town in Northeast Arkansas, his parents overcame incredible obstacles while he was yet a toddler, emerging through the instantaneous, delivering power of the Holy Spirit from a life of drugs, alcohol, parties and nightclubs and surging into a passionate and unwavering pursuit of the Lord and His Glory. He was raised on a church pew and in the altar where he heard for the first time at the age of seven the voice of the Lord calling him to minister the Gospel to a lost and dying world.

Jordan and his family held the pastorate in several churches in Arkansas, Oklahoma, Ohio and California and evangelized in many other churches regularly during his childhood and early adulthood. Ministry was life and served as the driving force for everything the Bradford family set their hands to do. Before the age of twenty-one, Jordan had served in multiple capacities on several ministry teams including associate pastor, executive pastor and youth pastor at various churches where his father served as senior pastor. He was also a member and co-director of church worship teams with his brother, Isaac, playing drums, lead guitar and bass guitar.

In the summer of 2007 Jordan was tragically burned in the construction of a youth center in Southeastern Ohio. He would later go on to name the center INFERNO Youth, which has reached countless young people with the message of Christ since that time. He suffered severe burns and was hospitalized in The Ohio State University burn unit in Columbus, Ohio. With fourth degree burns and the largest circumferential skin graft in the history of The Ohio State University Medical Center, Jordan's experience seemed tragic. The Lord, however, replaced tragedy with triumph, and before the end of Jordan's 21-day stay in the burn unit of OSU, he was unexpectedly visited by the head elder of World Harvest Church and Dean of World Harvest Bible College, Elder Ronnie Harrison. The Lord no doubt sent Ronnie Harrison that day on a specific mission to disenfranchise the enemy's plans for Jordan's life. He was given a full scholarship to World Harvest Bible College/Valor Christian College for the following semester. He registered for classes and was in attendance at WHBC/VCC that fall where he would lead in the music departments of the college, youth and church for the next two years.

It was through his burn that God began to open many doors for Jordan. In 2009 he was privileged to meet Grammy Award winning worship leader Israel Houghton. It was during this meeting, that Israel asked Jordan to speak at his annual worship conference, *A Deeper Level*, held in Houston, Texas. At the conference, Jordan spoke to countless people on an international platform about God's faithfulness and the power that **ONE** surrendered life can have on an entire generation.

In 2010, Jordan founded the Freedom for Appalachia Community Development Organization (FACDO), a nonprofit whose mission is to reach out to the young people of the Appalachian region. This burden was birthed while he was living and pastoring in Appalachia and encountered daily the poverty and challenges facing the young people who call it home. The organization is currently focusing its efforts on building a camp where homeless and disadvantaged youth can be housed as they are immersed in the Gospel and its principles for successful living. FACDO was founded as an educational organization, serving as a source of light and hope, providing opportunities to eradicate educational and social barriers that have plagued the region for generations.

Jordan understands very clearly the importance of submission to Godly authority and therefore sought out a ministry of integrity that would serve as a spiritual covering and source of guidance and wisdom. The Lord directed Jordan to the International Congress of Churches and Ministers, and today he is an Ordained Minister of the Gospel through ICCM under the leadership of Dr. Michael Chitwood. As he has continued to walk with the Lord and submit to His will, Jordan has had the opportunity to join forces with people of like faith and is highly regarded by Christian leaders all over the world. He has been involved in worship for several giants of the Faith, including Benny Hinn and Rod Parsley, and is in close fellowship with countless others, including Terry Tripp, Lawrence Bishop II and Chuck Lawrence.

Jordan and his brother Isaac are also co-founders of Bradford Ministries, a traveling ministry based in Nashville, Tennessee, and Judah Nation Band, a contemporary Christian worship band. JNB released its first EP in the summer of 2012 entitled, *No End*, and its songs are now being played both on radio stations and in churches. Jordan continues his work for the Lord as he travels with Bradford Ministries and Judah Nation Band to minister in churches and at conferences and conventions across the country through preaching, teaching and worship. He and his brother have also appeared on Daystar and TBN television programming.

The heart of that seven-year-old child still pounds within Jordan today to the rhythm of the heartbeat of God as he strives to fulfill no other calling than that placed upon him by his Creator and Savior. He is steadfast and strong in the plans of the Lord for what is to come *in* his life and *through* his life. No task is too difficult; no call is too high. Most certainly the Lord has raised him up for such a time as this, to lead a generation and display the Glory of the Lord as the time of His coming draws near.

One thing I ask from the Lord, this only do I seek: that I may dwell in the house of the Lord all the days of my life, to gaze on the beauty of the Lord and to seek him in his temple.

Psalm 27:4 (NLT)

Special Thanks

In the process of writing this book, there have been many people that have gone to great lengths and made great sacrifices to ensure that you would have the wealth of information contained within these pages. And without this very important section, those who have diligently served and sacrificed would remain nameless.

I would like to say a special thanks to my brother, Isaac Bradford, for his tireless pursuit in graphic design and his attention to detail, to my assistant, Mindy Chancey, for her tireless work in editing and compiling the information you are about to read, to Britnee Sauters for filling in all the gaps and always having a great attitude, and finally to all of the youth for which I have had the privilege of serving as youth pastor.

BRADFORDMINISTRIES
Touching The World With The Message Of Deliverance

As a ministry, we are committed to the educating and uplifting of the saints of God globally. Through the preached Word, worship evangelism, relief efforts, and the training up of the next generation of leadership by means of choir workshops and leadership incentives, our footprint on the earth is growing! We believe in the forward movement of the Church and its ability to reach the lost with the Gospel of Jesus Christ. It's up to us to make a lasting impact on this earth and touch the hurting, the broken and the bound with the message of deliverance. Learn more about our ministry and all of the available resources on our website!

WWW.BRADFORDMINISTRIES.NET

More Powerful Resources from

Jordan **Bradford**

Find out more about Jordan, his music, and his books at
www.bradfordministries.net

No End | EP

This 5-track ep was recorded in Los Angeles, California, and also in Cleveland
Tennessee, at *The Perry Stone Center Studio*. This ep is the first of many projects
to come by Jordan, Isaac and Judah Nation Band. All original Praise and Worship
songs birthed from real life experiences explode into a unique blend of gospel
rock and contemporary Christian. As a whole, this project captures a new sound
that is the heartbeat of this generation

TRACKS INCLUDE:
1. I Am Free
2. No End
3. Believe
4. Prophetic Decree
5. Alive In Me

Take Off Your Grave Clothes
TEACHING SERIES

This powerful audio message deals with the story of Lazarus in a never before seen light and reveals how it links to you today! This powerful sermon preached by Pastor Jordan Bradford will strengthen you in your journey!

You're Coming Out Without A Doubt!
TEACHING SERIES

Have you ever felt discouraged? If so, then this audio teaching by Pastor Jordan Bradford is for you! Life has a way of throwing us a curve ball and distracting us from our purpose which ultimately brings us down, but through this teaching you will discover how to believe again and bounce back from whatever life has thrown at you! Order this message TODAY!

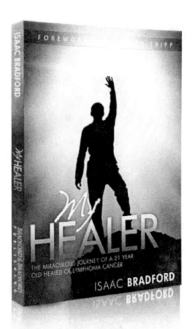

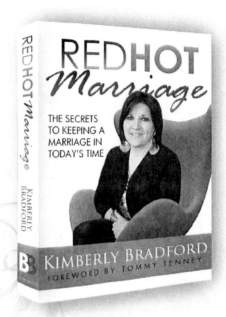

FOREWORD BY: TOMMY TENNEY

COMING SOON!

RED**HOT** *Marriage* is a must-read for all couples! Whether 'googily-eyed' over each other or sleeping in separate beds—you need this book. In today's society, divorce is at an all-time high, but that is not God's plan for you. The foundation of a long-lasting marriage that stands the test of time is one that starts with GOD. Using scripture and personal stories, Kimberly reveals the secrets of keeping a marriage in today's time. This book is for the happily married or those barely surviving. In this book you will learn:

- **How to overcome the temptation of divorce**
- **Sex begins at the altar**
- **How to revive ANY marriage!**

ABOUT THE AUTHOR - Kimberly Bradford is a mom, wife, and woman of God with an immense call on her life to speak and write about the greatness of our God. She has served in full-time ministry for over 20 years. Her ministry has impacted countless lives for the Gospel's sake. She now resides with her husband in Nashville, Tennessee.

FOR MORE INFO GO TO: BRADFORDMINISTRIES.NET/REDHOTMARRIAGE

GET THE LATEST PODCAST

 iTunes

We're here for you
24 hours a day online!

We want to be friends that you can count on. When you're far from home or simply needing the familiar voice of someone who cares, it's our hope that you will lean on this ministry and our resources for spiritual growth and affirmation. Our prayer for you is that the God of all grace anoints you with fresh oil, and His precious Spirit illuminates the Word in your life as you persevere through struggles and celebrate His abundance. When you visit our website to browse resources, read articles or watch our special videos, be sure to connect with us through Facebook, YouTube or Twitter!

Your
partnership with us makes a difference
in lives around the world

Everywhere around the world there are people who are desperate for the love of Christ in a real way. God continues to astound us with His power to heal, set free and bring deliverance to those who are bound. This ministry has been called by God in a new and fresh way to reach the lost and minister healing to those who are sick.

Whether it be the disadvantaged kids stranded in the mountains of Appalachia or the many thousands who attend conferences in the metroplexes of our cities, everyone needs ministry. Help us to reach more people than ever before with this powerful Gospel of HOPE. Your giving empowers us to administer healing to the broken. Without you, this would not be possible.

Thank you for *GIVING* - Thank you for *BELIEVING*

Jordan & Isaac Bradford

More info on back >

WE WANT
TO PRAY FOR YOU!

"IF TWO OF YOU AGREE
ON EARTH ABOUT ANYTHING
YOU ASK, IT WILL BE DONE
FOR YOU BY MY FATHER
IN HEAVEN.**"**

MATTHEW 18:19

PRAYER REQUESTS _____

_____

_____

_____

_____

_____

BM BRADFORDMINISTRIES
Touching The World With The Message Of Deliverance

BRADFORDMINISTRIES
Touching The World With The Message Of Deliverance

When you become a partner with Bradford Ministries, we enter into a covenant relationship with you. We know that as you sow into the awakening and re-generation that is taking place through Bradford Ministries, God will begin to awaken your children, your grandchildren, your youth group or church and the people of your region.

1. Giving Options Please Check One.

☐ **ONE TIME GIFT**
A one-time gift of any amount.

☐ **MINISTRY PARTNER**
A monthy gift of any amount

2. Personal Information

NAME

MAILING ADDRESS

CITY   STATE   ZIP

PHONE (optional)

EMAIL

3. Payment Information

☐ **CHECK OR MONEY ORDER $**_____
Please make checks payable to: Bradford Ministries (No C.O.D.s)

CREDIT CARD TYPE_____

CREDIT CARD #_____

EXP. DATE_____ / _____   CVC_____

SIGNITURE_____

We cannot process your request without your signiture or phone number. Thank you.
You can also donate on our secure website **BradfordMinistries.net**
For any further information call: **740-578-9572**